SEARCHING FOR GOD

Walk with God

Amos E Martinez

SEARCHING FOR GOD

SEEK AND YOU SHALL FIND

AMOS MARTINEZ

Writers Club Press

San Jose New York Lincoln Shanghai

SEARCHING FOR GOD
SEEK AND YOU SHALL FIND

Published by Writers Club Press
an imprint of iUniverse.com, Inc.

For information address:
iUniverse.com, Inc.
620 North 48th Street
Suite 201
Lincoln, NE 68504-3467
www.iuniverse.com

ISBN: 0-595-01117-9

Printed in the United States of America

CONTENTS

INTRODUCTION vii

Chapter 1   The Way to Come to God....................................3

Chapter 2   Religion And Government 13

Chapter 3   Comments About When Life Begins....................25

Chapter 4   Comments About The Trinity 33

Chapter 5   Comments About The Great Tribulation 39

Chapter 6   Comments About Heaven And Hell....................47

Chapter 7   Whom Shall We Call Father? 55

Chapter 8   Why Are There Many Denominations In Christianity?........61

Chapter 9   Does God Intervene In The Affairs Of Man 67

Chapter 10 King Of Kings And Lord Of Lords 75

Chapter 11 Government 85

Chapter 12 Politics 95

Chapter 13 Political Process..99

Chapter 14 The U. S. Constitution 101

Chapter 15   Treaties *113*

Chapter 16   Church And State...*115*

Chapter 17   Branches of Government......................................*119*

About the Author..*127*

About this Book..*129*

INTRODUCTION

Have you ever had a conversation about God and other things and said "I ought to write a book about that?" Well, I did. In fact this book covers several conversations. You might say, "I know all about that." Are you curious about what others say about what you believe? If so read on. This book may cover many of the subjects you discussed. Hopefully some new thoughts are brought out. After reading this book you may say "I could have done that." The fact is that you may have done a better job. But you didn't write a book. Hopefully you will enjoy reading about the many things you would have written about searching for God. The people in the conversations were not satisfied with what they had and were reaching for something. Hopefully, the information I gave helped satisfy that hunger and will help you with your witnessing.

It is interesting to note that none of the conversations were with people who claimed they were eminent scientists. Yet all of the people used the scientific method to arrive at their conclusions. That is to say that they had assimilated facts, researched their information, measured the data against what they understood to be a standard and felt confident about the subject they were discussing. This is no different from what you do. In fact, some say "It's about time someone other than an expert wrote a book about what the ordinary person is saying."

One of the first questions that comes to mind is, "Is there a God?" The question is addressed in the first chapter. Another question that then comes up is whether Jesus rose from the dead. Again you have to read the first chapter to address that issue. The conversations I have written about include talks with professors, business leaders, individuals in various professions and crafts, clergy and others. There are a wide variety of opinions and every opinion is compared with what is found in the King James translation of the Bible. Whenever there is a conflict between man's knowledge and the scriptures, I have chosen to believe the scriptures rather than man's wisdom. I hope this book confirms your understanding of the scriptures and helps you to be a better witness of the gospel of Jesus Christ.

What other interesting topics were brought up? The table of contents will give you a good idea about topics discussed. I have categorized conversations into chapters in Section I and treated each subject as if it were a chapter.

Also it must be pointed out that the author is not a sexist. The use of the term "him" or "his" means "her" and "hers" as appropriate. In other words gender is not limited to male only. I shouldn't have to explain this but in this "political correct" environment such an explanation is appropriate lest someone be offended.

Section II, beginning in Chapter 11, is based on research rather than conversations. Consider that politics, the political process and government are three distinct institutions rather than one. Because they are three institutions rather than one I have called it the Unholy Trinity.

All scripture quotations are from the King James version.

I

SEARCHING FOR GOD

1

THE WAY TO COME TO GOD

As you begin to read this and the following chapters imagine that you are hearing conversations about the various topics. I want you to experience the same feelings that you might get if you were actually listening in. So enjoy yourself and hear what others are saying as they search for God

IS THERE A GOD?

The first thing we have to establish is whether there is a God at all. This is a subject about which there were so many conversations, I hardly know where to begin. There are many scriptures that lead one to conclude that there is a God. The Bible mentions God 3,893 times. Genesis 1:1 starts off by saying that **God** created the heaven and the earth. In fact much of Genesis refers to God. Then we can go to John 1:1 which states "In the beginning was the Word, and the Word was with **God**, and the Word was **God**." The conversations invariably led to discussions of whether there are more than one way to come to God. All of the conversations had one thing in common.

Everyone was looking for a way to get to heaven. This led to other questions such as where is heaven and what is it like.

COMMENTS ABOUT HEAVEN AND HELL

Some people thought we were already in heaven. Others wanted to get there but didn't want to die in the process. Still others believed there is no heaven and that we just keep getting better with each life until we reach unity with God. It is interesting to note what many people thought about heaven. What do you think? Later on I will quote some things that the Bible has to say about the subject. Many Christians have encountered these types of conversations about heaven. Hopefully this book will reaffirm some thoughts about heaven and will help you the next time someone asks you about heaven.

We have already tackled the question as to whether there is a God or not.

II Timothy 3:16 which says in part, "All scripture is given by the inspiration of God..." To me this tells me two things. First that there is a God. And second, that He gave us the word by His inspiration.

IS GOD MALE OR FEMALE?

Having established that there is a God, the conversation turned to as to whether God is a male or a female. John 4:24 says, "God is a spirit: and those that worship Him must worship Him in spirit and in truth." Some say a spirit is neither male nor female. Thus, the question remains is God a male or a female? Did not Jesus refer to the Father God? In John 3:37 Jesus says that the Father sent Him. We get more into the subject of Father in chapter 7. Suffice it here to say that father refers to a male. Therefore we can say with confidence that God is a male.

COMING TO GOD

Having settled that there is a God and that He is a male, we next turn to the question of how to come to Him. Some say there are many ways. Chief among the analogies made to me was the one of many rivers flowing to the sea. It was said that anyone sailing on the River of Christianity would sail to the sea. Someone else sailing on the river of another religion would sail to the same sea. Therefore comparing religions to rivers leads one to the conclusion that there are many ways to get to the Father and to heaven.

This concept bears further examination. Ecclesiastics 1:7 states that "all rivers run to the sea: yet the sea is not full; unto the place from whence the rivers came, thither they return again." Observation reveals that the sun heats the sea. Moisture rises up and is carried by the wind to the north where it condenses and falls as rain or snow in the places where the rivers begin. The cycle starts all over again.

JUDGMENT

The Bible says that man returns to dust from whence he came. Thus it seems that man's life can be compared to the water in the rivers. The comparison ends there as man does not start over again. There was much discussion regarding man's beginning again after death. This theory is reincarnation with a different twist. It was thought that man comes back and gets better each time until he reaches unity with God. However, according to Hebrews 9:27 which says, "And as it is appointed unto man once to die, but after this the judgment." It seems that man unlike the rivers, does not begin the cycle all over again. After death man is judged and dispatched to one of two destinations. From this one might conclude that good works are all that is needed to be dispatched to the more favorable place.

Not so. Good works do count for something but what causes one to do good works? Some people are so heavenly minded that they are no earthly good. There needs to be an occupation on earth until Jesus returns. Part of that occupation involves doing good works. Good works are the result of being obedient to the Creator. One cannot be disobedient and serve the Lord at the same time.

ENOUGH IS ENOUGH

It is interesting to note that man-made religions try to make Christian theology accept many of the thoughts that are contrary to the teachings in the Bible. Most man-made religions make one feel good because they make out that a loving God has mercy and grace for everything. Later on we will talk about mercy and grace and the difference between the two. They neglect the fact that God passes righteous judgment on everything. Though He is long suffering and will not zap us right away when we go astray, He offers the right path but at the end there is judgment. One has only to look at the cities of Sodom and Gomorrah and at the people around the Tower of Babel to see that God finally says enough is enough.

JESUS, THE SON OF GOD

But this gets us away from the subject. Let me quote John 6:44 which states in part that Jesus said, "No man can come to me, except the Father which has sent me draw him..." Elsewhere we conclude that Jesus is the son of God, therefore no one can come to God except through Jesus. So much for the theory that there are many ways to come to God. Sailing a river other than Christianity may get you to the sea but not to God and heaven. Unlike the water which returns from whence the rivers came, death comes and judgment is passed. We don't get a chance to start all over again. Thus today is the day to make Jesus the Lord of your life and accept salvation.

SALVATION

Unlike natural things we purchase, salvation is free. We can't do good works or otherwise earn it. It is a gift from God but it is conditioned upon repentance and acceptance of the Father through faith. As mentioned elsewhere in the book, man does have the free will to accept or reject God. This freedom and obedience or lack thereof is discussed further when predestination is mentioned.

BIBLE, THE WORD OF GOD

They say that the Bible is not the complete word. They say that scientists have discovered many things which prove the Bible to be incomplete. For this I refer to Deuteronomy 4:2 which reads in part, "Ye shall not add unto the word which I have commanded you, neither shall you diminish ought from it…" There are many books which contain information that is not in the Bible but they do not add to the word of God. For instance, I studied many books to learn about radio theory and the Morse Code to become an amateur radio operator. The Bible did not contain this information. However, the radio waves were created by God a long time ago. It took man a long time to discover and make use of them but they were there all along. Man then mastered them and today it would be difficult to live without such a wonderful creation. A long time ago I desired in my heart to become an amateur radio operator. The Lord then used it and led me to provide communications between a missionary and the states. This is to say that the desire of the heart is mans but the steps are ordered by the Lord. I never imagined when I desired to become an amateur radio operator that I would provide vital communications between Guatemala and the states for the Lord's work. I just mentioned one incident but there are others. The point I am trying to illustrate is that there are many good books but they don't add to the Word of God. They merely describe something that man has discovered. The feature was there all along, placed there by God before the formation of the earth but recently discovered by man. The radio waves were always there but it wasn't until recent times that man discovered how to use them. The same is true of other "inventions." Man writes many wonderful books to describe how to operate such "inventions" but those books do not add to the Word of God. With regards to man's knowledge I look at Proverbs 14:12 which says, "There is a way which seemeth right unto a man, but the end thereof are the ways of death." Then follow up with Proverbs 21:2 which says, "Every way of a man is right in his own eyes but the Lord ponders the heart." To this add Ecclesiastes 1:2 which states, "Vanity of vanities, saith the preacher, vanity of vanities; all is vanity." This is to say that men give credit to mankind for the things God has created.

There are many more scriptures along this vain but the point is that man's knowledge does not enhance the Word of God. Man's knowledge is very limited compared with God's wisdom. Look around at nature. You just know that man cannot do such wonderful things and that they didn't happen by accident.

EVIDENCE OF RESURRECTION

Another question that then comes up is whether we can believe that Jesus rose from the dead. For this I begin by looking at the evidence presented by Paul in I Corinthians 15:3 through 7 which reads beginning in verse 3, "For I delivered unto you first of all that which I also received, how that Christ died for our sins according to scriptures;" and continues in verse 4, "And that He was buried, and rose again the third day according to the scriptures:" Paul is talking about the evidence presented in the scriptures. He goes on to say that if you don't believe the scriptures then ask someone who saw Jesus after He arose. In verse 5 he presents further evidence in that the verse says, "And after that He was seen of Cephas, then of the twelve:" He goes on to say that others saw Him for verse 6 says, "After that, He was seen of above five hundred brethren at once; of whom the greater part remain unto this present, but some are fallen asleep." Then he goes on to say that James and the apostles saw Him. Verse 7 says, "After that, He was seen of James; then of all the apostles." And he concludes with the evidence that he saw Him also as he says in verse 8 that, "And last of all He was seen of me also, as one born out of due time.

LOGIC

In addition to presenting evidence he appeals to logic in I Corinthians 15:12-22. He finds it illogical to preach that He rose from the dead and yet contend that there is no resurrection. Verse 12 says, "Now if Christ be preached that He rose from the dead, how say some among you that there is no resurrection of the dead." He emphasizes this in verse 13, "But if there is no resurrection of the dead, then is Christ not risen." He goes on to say that our preaching is in vain and our faith is also in vain if Christ is not risen. Verse 14 clearly states that with the statement, "And if Christ be not risen, then is our preaching in vain, and your faith is also in vain." Adding to the logic Paul says we are false witnesses if we testify Jesus is risen and contend that the dead rise not. Verse 15 reads, "Yea, and we are found false witness of God; because we have testified of God that He raised up Christ: Whom He raised not up, if so be that the dead rise not."

He continues the logical trend in verse 16 which says, "For if the dead rise not, then is not Christ raised:" and completes the thought in verse 17. "And if Christ be not raised, your faith is vain: ye are yet in your sins." If Jesus died for our sins how can we yet be in our sins? In verses 18 and 19 he tells us in a sense that we should play golf, go boating, and otherwise enjoy life. Giving up these things will make you miserable if you *have* to assemble yourself to praise him. At least that is the impression I get when I read, "Then they also which are fallen asleep in Christ are perished." and "If in this life only we have hope in Christ, we are of all men most miserable." Some people are miserable because they *have* to attend church. However, followers of Christ *want* to assemble themselves with other Christians. One place where you can assemble yourself with Christians is church.

CONTINUED LOGIC

Continuing with logic we have verse 20, "But now is Christ risen from the dead, and become the first fruits of them that slept." (If there are first fruits, there must be second fruits and so on.) More will be said about other fruits later. However, for now let's concentrate on resurrection as described in the first part of verse 20 which gives us logical hope that we too will be resurrected. The thought of man's resurrection is further bolstered by verse 21 which reads, "For since by man came death, by man came also the resurrection of the dead." Christ makes this all possible in spite of Adam's fall because "For as in Adam all die, even so in Christ shall all be made alive." (I Corinthians 15:22)

This is a long dissertation on Paul's presenting evidence and logic but I think this proves that Jesus rose from the dead. At least that answers the question for me. I realize that we no longer can ask some of the people that saw Jesus if they actually saw Him. However, there is no reason not to rely on the scriptures because they were given by the inspiration of God. To deny the truthfulness of the scriptures is to call God a liar. It says in John 11:25 that Jesus said He is the resurrection. That is good enough for me.

So far we have established that there is a God, that He is male, that there is only one way to come to Him, and that Jesus rose from the dead. It is important that we keep these principles in mind as we read the other chapters. These principles help us to understand the conversations and the Biblical perspective on various topics.

GENDER

I know that it is politically correct to make gender a neutral item when referring to religious beliefs. There are many churches revising their hymnals to eliminate any references to male and female. It is said that there will be a Bible translation where gender will be neutral. However, it was not that way in the beginning. Genesis 1:27 states that God created male and female. Thus I see no reason not to call someone a male and someone else of the opposite sex a female. What some denominations and the new Bible version are doing may be politically correct but is it scripturally correct? Going back to the statement that God gave us the Word by His inspiration one would have to conclude that He intended for there to be a male and a female. To contend otherwise is to call Him a liar.

JESUS, THE ONLY WAY

With the realization that there is a God and that He is a male we come back to the issue of many ways to come to God. We have already stated that Jesus said there is only one way to come to the Father. It may sound like I am repeating myself but I want to emphasize that there is only one way to come to the Father. In addition to saying that Jesus said so we have also shot down the theory of many rivers and religions flowing to the sea to prove that there are many ways to come to the Father.

GOOD WORKS

Another theory holds that one can get to heaven by doing good works. We have already pointed out that good works count for something in the judgment that takes place. However, good works are not to be equated with brownie points. By placing all bets on works one denies God. At least that is the interpretation I get when I read Titus 1:16 which says, "They profess that they know God; but in works they deny him, being abominable, and disobedient, and unto every good work reprobate." There are many more scriptures which point out that man is not justified by works but I can't cover them all in this chapter. Faith is an element that helps one to be justified but that is another subject and we will not address that now. However, we will state that man is not justified by works and contend that theory, like the one about many rivers, is not valid.

What are we left with? I guess we can safely say that there are not many ways to come to God. If there are not many ways, is there just one way? None of my conversations led me to understand that there is another way. In fact, my conversations convinced me that there is only one way to come to God and that is through Jesus.

ONE WAY

The one way theory is not so strange when one looks around at natural things. Whoever heard that three parts of hydrogen and one part oxygen make water? There is only one formula for water and so it is for many other things. There is only one way to get to many things. Not only is there only one way but the proportion of elements must be combined in exact quantities. Thus the theory of one way to come to God is easily equated with other *one way* activity. No, we cannot say that *one way* is harsh. It is the only way to accomplish certain things.

MERCY AND GRACE

Earlier it was said that there would be further discussion on mercy and grace. One simple way to look at it is to say that with mercy we get what we deserve. With grace we don't get what we deserve. One way to illustrate this is to say that we all deserve to go to hell but by God's grace we don't go there. All we have to do is ask for salvation and it is there for free. There is only one way to come to the Father, and that is through his Son. It is only through God's grace and mercy that we are saved.

2

RELIGION AND GOVERNMENT

There seems to be a misconception about politics, the political process, and government. I call it the unholy trinity because the three are not one. I like to think of this chapter as Civics 101 1/2. The half they didn't teach you in school. I'll try to make this interesting as well as informative. According to Romans 13:1 "…all the powers that be are ordained by God." I'll begin by talking about government.

PURPOSE OF GOVERNMENT

One of the main purposes of government is to see that things are done decently and in order. Politics on the other hand does things indecently and out of order. More on this when we discuss politics. The political process is the vehicle we use to get into government or politics. God ordained government. Somebody else ordained politics. Man figured out that we need the political process to get either into politics or into government.

CHRISTIANS AND GOVERNMENT

Many people say that Christians should not be involved in politics. I agree with that statement. I believe Christians should be involved in government and not in politics. The current political situation is such that it is almost considered a crime for Christians to express an interest in the affairs of their civil government. We hear the statement that there is a separation of church and state. It was never the intent of our founding fathers to deny religion. Their intent was only to deny state sponsorship of any religion.

RELIGION AND GOVERNMENT

There are many good books dispelling the notion that religion and government do not mix so I won't go into detail on that account. Suffice it to say that the constitution guarantees us freedom of religion, not freedom from religion. The term religion has a different connotation today than it did when the constitution was written. Then the word religion was associated with the word Christianity. Now-a-days the word religion can be associated with the New Age Movement, with Islam, with Christianity, etc. We are not here to discuss religion but rather the role of Christianity in government.

CHRISTIAN PARTICIPATION

First of all, I would like to quote Patrick Henry who said, "It cannot be emphasized too strongly or too often that this great nation was not founded by religionists but by Christians. Not on religion but on the gospel of Jesus Christ." To emphasize the role of religion in our civil government I quote John Quincy Adams who went on to say, "The highest glory of the American revolution was this: that it connected in one indissoluble bond, the principles of civil government with the principles of Christianity." Thus it cannot be emphasized too strongly or too often that Christians should be involved in government and not in politics.

CHRISTIAN FOUNDATION OF U.S. GOVERNMENT

Many religions proclaim that the role of government is to insure peace, justice and prohibit acts such as murder, slander, etc. Thus some people contend that our government is based on the principles of many religions including Christianity. Is this a Christian nation or not? A study by Baylor University revealed that 34 percent of the quotations in the constitution came directly from the Bible. The other 66 percent were from people who were quoting men that quoted the Bible. Thus we can say that this is a Christian nation. There are some prominent leaders who believe this nation was founded on deist, not Christian principles. True, some of the founding fathers were deists but why did they quote the Bible in the constitution and not some other book? Is there any doubt that quoting the Bible makes this a Christian nation? According to Barna Research Group, Oxnard, California, statistics say that 93% of Americans believe in God.

BRANCHES OF GOVERNMENT

And even if their statements were true, there is no denying the fact that religious beliefs influence civil government. The question is whose religion? We are talking here about the U.S. Government. The constitution and the bill of rights (part of the constitution) govern, or should govern, the actions of our government. To refresh your memory I will point out that the constitution sets up three branches of the federal government. And where does the idea of three branches of government come from? If you will look in the Bible you will find that there were kings, judges and God gave us laws or legislated. Does this not sound like executive, judicial and legislative branches? True, the Book of Judges is the history of Israel during the times of the fifteen judges. This makes it look like there is only one branch of government. Still, there had to be a law giver, executor, and a judge. One has to embrace the concept and not just look at the Book of Judges.

CHANGE IN THE CONSTITUTION?

Thus one can say that our system of civil government **was** based on Christian principles. I use the term **was** because many people content that it **is** not. The fact of the matter is that there needs to be a change. Should we update the constitution or should we change our attitude and go back to its original intent? The original intent seems to promote that things are done decently and in order. Things at the present time seem to be indecent and out of order. If this is the case, we need to change our attitude. The constitution has served us well and can continue to do so if we change our attitude.

POLITICAL PARTIES

Consider political parties. The constitution is silent about such organizations. In this country we have many parties. Two parties have emerged as the dominant parties. Thus we can say that the two party system is at work in this country. One need only to look around the world to see that coalition governments have not done as well as the two party system in the U.S.

Considering only the two major political parties, one can conclude that becoming a part of a party becomes the way to inject one's views into government. Many people believe that the parties are controlled by "cliques." Not so. You can get in on the ground floor of political parties by offering your services. Attend one of their meetings and take an active interest in its activities. Make it known that you are willing to work. Accept responsibility on floor work and on committees. Soon you will get the hang of things and will be in a position to help determine who will represent the party at election time. You'd be surprised at how little time it takes but it is time well spent. To paraphrase a saying I will say, "Ask not what your party can do for you, ask what you can do for your party."

POLITICAL PROCESS

It is clear then that the political process can get one involved in government. If you are not careful, it can get you involved in politics. You want to be involved with or in government and not with or in politics. In this case ask not what your government can do for you but rather what can you do for your government. Remember that in the U.S., government only has the authority granted to it by the people. It is fair to say that the person (people) who pays the fiddler calls the tune. Thus government is to be the people's servant, not its master.

MASTER OR SERVANT?

Does the government serve the people or do the people serve the government? This is why it is important to have the political process express the will of the people. The framers of the constitution said that this was a government by the people and for the people. They were aware that when government was the master rather than the servant of the people bad things happened. Thus a government controlled by the people is a process that serves them. The framers even provided a means of amending the constitution to ensure that government reflected the will of the people to have things done decently and in order.

The political process offers people the opportunity to become involved in the workings of government. Many individuals have used the process to advance themselves rather than the good of society. Thus we have politicians rather than statesmen running the government. We can then go on to examine politics and compare it to government.

POLITICAL PROCESS, NOT POLITICS

The political process clearly is not to be confused with politics. As noted earlier, the political process enables one to become involved with government or politics. Remember that we are trying to establish the fact that government, politics and the political process are three distinct elements. We want to eliminate politics from government. Politics is a counterfeit to good government.

Let's review the upside and downside of politics. The upside leaves a lot to be desired and the downside has a disastrous effect on the governed.

One can say that the upside has a short term benefit while the downside affects the governed for a long time.

First the upside. Certain individuals use the political process to enhance or enlarge their ego. They promise everything to everyone. You are familiar with people who will say anything to please you. It is no wonder people will have second thoughts about what a politician says. For a long time we have observed politicians who talk the talk but don't walk the walk. If it sounds too good to be true, it probably is not true. The conclusion can only be that the upside is only for the politician and not for the governed.

Looking at the downside can take the rest of this book but suffice it to look at a couple of instances. First Let's talk about things being done indecently. One need only to look at the national debt. The size of the debt is due to politicians giving us goodies and passing the cost onto our children and grandchildren. We are as much to blame as the politicians for this condition. After all, the politicians got and stayed in office through our vote or lack thereof. It is doubtful that anyone views the size of the national debt as decent. There are many more examples of indecent acts by our government but the bottom line is that we the people have a responsibility for the operation of the government.

Now Let's look at something out of order. Again we can only point to one item among the many. One of the functions of government is to provide a safe environment. One area of safety has to do with protection against harmful actions. An area of harmful actions is certain sexual behavior and certain criminal activity. Government action is out of order in offering protection for sexual behavior while at the same time taking away the means of protection against criminal activity. More specific, the government is handing out condoms to protect against unsafe sex and taking away guns so one cannot protect oneself against criminal activity. Laws are passed to take guns off the street but end up taking guns away from those who would use guns to protect themselves. This clearly is government doing things out of order. One can make a long list of things government does out of order. Many of the things seem right and perhaps are right in the short run but clearly put the cart before the horse.

SHORT RUN, LONG RUN

It has been said that the only thing that matters is the short run because in the long run we are all dead! It is true that we may be dead in the long run but do we want to spoil the long run for our children and grandchildren? We will if we continue to let government do things out of order.

CHRISTIAN PRINCIPLES

This brings us back to the proposition that Christians should be involved in government and not in politics. Christian principles ensure that government does things decently and in order. One need only to look in the Bible to see what these things are. There are people who contend that the principles of good government found in the Bible promote intolerance, divisiveness, war, etc. Not so. The Bible merely points out practices that are acceptable and unacceptable. The unacceptable practices lead some to conclude that Christians are intolerant and bigoted.

Of course Christians do not endorse the kind of behavior mentioned in the Bible as unacceptable. Some say that if a specific word is not used in the Bible then that specific behavior is not prohibited or seen as unacceptable. Further Christians who contend that the specific behavior is not acceptable are said to be intolerant. Clearly those who are out of bounds take issue with those who are in bounds. To declare certain activity to be out of bounds based on the rule book does not make one intolerant.

BOUNDARIES

The Bible and the laws of the government declare murder as clearly unacceptable. We do not see opposition to murder as an intolerable act. Yet such behavior clearly puts a boundary around what a would-be murderer can do. Are both the Bible and the government intolerant in this case? What is the difference between pointing out that someone is out of bounds in this case and other situations declared unacceptable by Biblical standards? How come it does not make one intolerant in this case but intolerant in pointing out other out of bound situations? One can clearly see that the word intolerant does not apply to situations that point to out of bounds behavior in our society.

CONSTITUTION FOR GODLY PEOPLE

These Christian principles following the gospel of Jesus Christ are clearly applicable to governmental actions. Many of the principles are incorporated into the U.S. constitution. The constitution does not attempt to micro-manage our lives. Rather it sets out a range of principles which guide us and ensures that things are done decently and in order. The constitution was not intended for an ungodly people. No amount of laws based on the constitution can change one's heart. First one must embrace Christian principles for our form of government to work. This is true whether in the U.S. or elsewhere in the world.

What good does a law prohibiting murder do if the heart of someone is intent in murdering somebody? Obviously the murderer is not abiding by the commandment, "Thou shall not murder." If the murderer has not taken the word of God, what chance is there that he will take the word of government? So we see that indeed the constitution is not for those who are ungodly.

GODLY LAWS

What chance is there for there for ungodly men to enact Godly laws? It is therefore incumbent on Christians to see that Godly people are elected to positions in government. Christians therefore have an obligation to participate in civil government. Thus if Christians are involved in the affairs of government one will have to agree that religion and government do mix. This is in direct opposition to the statement that there should be a separation of church and state.

As was stated earlier, there are many good books that examine this concept and we will not examine the issue other than to say that the gospel of Jesus Christ influenced our founding fathers. The concept of "Separation of Church and State" is nowhere mentioned in the constitution. The wall or separation mentioned by Jefferson has been taken out of context. The separation was to say that government did not control the church and that the church did not control the government. It is one thing for the church to control government, it is quite another thing for Christian principles to be embodied in governmental affairs.

MENTIONING CHRISTIAN BELIEFS

Thus there is nothing wrong with churches mentioning governmental affairs when proclaiming the gospel of Jesus Christ. It is quite another thing for government to intrude or prohibit Christian religious activities. We have arrived at a time when courts place heavy emphasis on the establishment clause while ignoring the prohibition clause in the constitution. It is abundantly clear that the government shall not establish a national religion. It should also be abundantly clear that the government is not to prohibit the free exercise thereof. Shouldn't we view the prohibition of the mention of God in public places as a prohibition to the free exercise of religious beliefs? There is no doubt that many public officials and others have misinterpreted the constitution.

BIBLES VERSUS GUNS

For example, some judges contend that the court has not prohibited prayer in school. Yet many school officials have interpreted various court actions as prohibiting Christian students from praying or even bringing a Bible to school. Bringing a Bible to some schools is treated the same as bringing a gun. Are a Bible and a gun equivalent? The constitution gives one the right to bear arms but does not say that one does have the right to bear a Bible. Stretching this illogical conclusion one can say that it is OK to bring a gun to school but not a Bible. It is this kind of reasoning that has put us on a slippery slope to bad results. For this reason it is important that Christians take to heart the admonition to occupy until Jesus returns. What better way to occupy than to be active in government. Participation can range from voting to running for office and everything in between.

Thus, one can find many scriptures in Christianity urging participation in government. As stated before, God ordained government, someone else ordained politics. In His ordaining government He gave us some responsibility for participating in running such affairs. Politics is an imitation of government. (A counterfeit if you will.) We have been brainwashed into thinking that politics and government are the same. Again, a reminder that Christians are not to be involved in "politics." There is very much to do in government.

EXPERIENCE

Earlier we mentioned how to become part of a political party. One of the things not elaborated on is the fact that this is one way to learn what is expected of an elected official. The experience gained outside of government may give one the necessary experience needed to serve in local, state, or national positions. However, the Lord needs to call one to such a job. Remember that we have a good reason to hold fast to our profession. Not only are we to profess Jesus Christ but we are to do everything as unto the Lord. Thus in whatever we do we are to glorify Him. Where do you think you can give Him glory, in politics or in government?

RELIGION AND GOVERNMENT

You will notice that this chapter is headed religion and government, not church and government. We want you to make the distinction between church and religion. You will see that religion has an important role to play in government. As stated earlier, the framers of the constitution equated religion with Christianity. That was a handy convenience. The word religion is not necessarily associated with Christianity today. Today it is probably more appropriate to say the gospel of Jesus Christ rather than religion. The word religion may include false doctrines as well as the word of God. There is salvation in God and there is only *one* way to come to Him. Having read this chapter one can only conclude that religion and government do mix. It is probably more proper to say that the gospel of Jesus Christ needs to be followed if we are to have good government.

PARTICIPATION IN GOVERNMENT

Thus this book and the Bible point out responsibilities of Christians for active participation in civil government. It has been said that all that is needed for evil to prevail is for good people to remain silent. For too long Christians have remained silent when it comes to operating government programs. In fact many leaders have urged Christians not to become involved in civil government. It is this silence that has enabled those in government to make unnecessary bad laws. Christian involvement in government is appropriate if government is to be run according to the gospel of Jesus Christ.

3

WHEN DOES LIFE BEGIN?

It should be stated at the beginning that medical science and the legal profession do not agree on when life begins. Therefore discussions on this subject ranged all the way from saying that life begins at conception to life beginning when a live delivery takes place. You probably have heard all of these discussions and have arrived at some conclusion. We will examine these opinions based on logic and what the Bible says about the subject.

LIFE BEGINS AT BIRTH

To begin with let's examine the contention that life begins upon delivery. This assumes that life did not exist prior to delivery. Logic would lead one to conclude that if this is the case then a lifeless thing was somehow growing even though it was dead. The thing could grow because the woman carrying it was alive. The thing didn't turn out to be an animal because biology teaches us that each species propagates their own kind. An exception to this "law" is the birth of a mule which is a hybrid between a horse and a donkey. Since man and woman are not affected by this happenstance, a child is formed.

NEW LIFE

The birth of a child results in a new life according to this belief. Somehow delivery brings life to a previously dead thing. Thus, life begins at birth (delivery). This is possible because God can make something out of nothing. In this case there is something with two legs, two arms, and all the other features of a human that is brought to life. God takes a dead thing and gives it life. Some would contend that a woman giving birth gives life. The issue here is not who gives life but rather when does life begin. This conversation led to a conclusion that could not be supported in the end. Thus, **life** begins sometime before delivery. But when?

BACKING UP TO FIND LIFE

We will explore that issue as well as others as we continue. How far back from delivery does one have to go to find life? That is the question of the day. Is a fetus alive? Even the courts have not ruled consistently on that issue. Take for example the case of a mother who was accused of killing her baby in the womb because she did not take reasonable care of herself. Then there is the case of a man convicted of double murder when he shot a woman who was pregnant. Yet the courts have ruled that elective abortion is not murder. Such double standards are the fault of the laws and not the courts.

LEGISLATIVE PROCESS

It is important for the public to see to it that the laws are consistent. How does the public see to this? The price of liberty is eternal vigilance. Thus it is important to pay attention to what candidates say and then watch what they do once in office. This is a slow legislative process but it must be followed if there is to be agreement between the law and medicine as to when life begins. Don't lose sight of the fact that there is disagreement between the law and the medical profession as to when life begins. However, even the medical profession is not immune from the law. More on this later.

ALIVE

Back to conversations on when life begins. Another conversation backed the beginning of life from delivery to the first kick felt by a mother. After all John kicked when Mary saluted Elisabeth. That is a sure sign that there was life when John recognized the presence of Jesus in Mary's womb. While this theory has more validity than the conversation that life begins at delivery it also lacks an explanation of how a dead object can grow as well as having other deficiencies.

Before we address those deficiencies Let's hear some more about this conversation. To begin with, it went something like this. The first sign of life is when a baby gives its first kick. According to this theory abortion after the first kick is murder. Many people can agree with that but is that when life begins? Logic would lead one to conclude that there must be some kind of living organism to give that limb the ability to give a kick.

FROM DEATH TO LIFE

The person who advanced this theory was of the opinion that prior to the first kick the organism was developing but had no life. The terms "developing" and "no life" seem to contradict each other. Have you ever seen a "dead" thing "develop?" There must be some kind of power or "life" for development to take place. It was said that the power behind this development was the mother's life. This was traced to the mother's action in growing the "thing" inside her tummy. However, this does not take into account the fact that there is a separate beating heart in the "thing." How do we know there is a separate beating heart? Medical science tells us that this is the case. If it is said that life begins with the first kick then the small beating heart must be dead. The logic of this conclusion escapes the writer.

WHICH TRIMESTER?

This leads the writer to conclude that life began sometime before the first kick. This was one of the deficiencies noted about this theory. If we can back up this far and say that life began before this time how far can we back up? Can we say that life begins three weeks after conception? What's to keep us from saying two weeks or one week? As you can see, we can just keep on trucking until one hits the beginning. What then is the beginning? Is it at conception or before? After all, God said that before He formed thee in the belly He knew thee. Does this apply only to Jeremiah or does this apply to all of us? Does this mean that life can begin before we are conceived? Let's examine this a little further.

LIFE BEFORE CONCEPTION?

In view of the writing of Jeremiah there is no doubt that the Word of the Lord came to him. God had a definite plan for Jeremiah and He told him about it. This leads us to conclude that He knows all before conception. In Jeremiah 1:5 the Lord says in part, "Before I formed you in the womb I knew you;…" Does it follow than that life begins before conception? No. With God being all-knowing means He knows those things which do not have life as well as those things which do have life. This means that He can know us even before we have life. This still leaves us with the question of when does life begin.

FLESH AND SPIRIT

Let's look at some other clues. Does the Bible not say that what is born of the flesh is flesh? Natural birth involves some kind of birth other than the born again experience. Jesus was referring to the spirit in John 3. There is agreement that the living body has flesh. Therefore the kind of life we are talking about involves the flesh and not the spirit. Telling us that the body is flesh does not tell us when life begins. However, flesh must have blood running through it to keep it alive. There must be some kind of pump to make the blood run. We refer to that pump as a heart. We've heard that abortion stops a beating heart. This book is not about abortion but it will acknowledge that there needs to be a beating heart in order for there to be life. Thus we have concluded at this time that life begins sometime before delivery.

HEART BEATS

Does it follow then that life begins when the heart begins beating? This is part of the solution to the question of when does life begin. It is a little bit like putting a puzzle together. Most of us know that a puzzle is not complete until the last piece is in place. We have not put the last piece in place to the question of when does life begin.

Let's review what we have found to date. It was noted that life began sometime before delivery. It was also noted that there had to be life before the first kick. It was further noted that the body contained flesh. We established that there must be the capacity for blood to circulate in that flesh to sustain life. We said that it was necessary to have a beating heart in order for there to be running blood. Thus we have established a basis for the beginning of life but we have not concluded when life begins.

We're working our way to that point. We just have to work our way back to what we'll call the beginning. Everything has a beginning, middle, and end. Believe me, the conversation touched on all three aspects but we are only concerned with beginning in this chapter. The other aspects were interesting and they are covered in another book but for now we want to address only the beginning. Hang in there and you will see what these conversations concluded after much discussion and thought. Note that we backed up to the point where we detected that blood was flowing. After all, it is said that life is in the blood. Does this explain the beginning of life? We're almost there but we have to ask is this really the beginning?

LIFE BEGINS AT CONCEPTION

Congressman Glenn Poshard says he believes that life begins at conception. Biology stipulates that an egg must be fertilized before there can be life. Does such an event take place at conception? Most fair minded people believe that a woman's egg is fertilized at conception. That explanation would lead one to conclude that human life begins at conception. Although the conversation was not with Congressman Glenn Poshard, the conclusion was the same as his. Your conclusion may or may not be the same. If it is different, check your biology and the Bible.

True that the Bible does not state "life begins at conception." However reading and understanding what the Holy Spirit imparts one can clearly arrive at the conclusion that other than Adam and Eve, life begins at conception. More could be said about this but the bottom line is that logic and prayer leads to such a conclusion. You probably have heard all this before but this might add to your thought about the subject.

Let's consider the concept of life beginning at conception a little further. We have logically eliminated all other time. We did this by going back to each position and concluded that life began sometime prior to the stated event or time. Finally we backed up to the time of conception. The basis for this was biological and Biblical. One of the Biblical passages dealing with conception is Genesis 16:4 when a woman conceived a child after Abram went into Hagar. There are many scriptures stating that a man and a woman can conceive a child. Many people wish to eliminate the Bible, not because they don't believe the Bible but because they don't believe those who base their case solely on the Bible.

BIOLOGY

Recognizing this and the fact that the Bible and biology come to the same conclusion nevertheless we will stick with biology because the conversations were along those lines. Any biology book will confirm the fact that an egg must be fertilized in order for a growth to take place. How about in vitro fertilization? Such fertilization takes place *outside* of the mother's womb. There can even be division of cells in certain embryos. But is there blood? The Bible says that life is in the blood. The Bible also says that conception takes place *inside* the mother's womb. In vitro fertilization takes place *outside* the mother's womb. Such fertilization often results in multiple births again proving that man is not in control. Further any biology book will affirm that each specie reproduces its kind. Thus, for there to be human life there must be conception in the mother's womb. Prior to that there can be all kinds of thoughts and feelings but nothing happens until conception in the mother's womb. From that time on there is some kind of new life. Some say that a fetus comes into being and if it is not aborted then a child is born. Regardless of what that "something" is called, a new life begins when the egg is fertilized in the natural way or implanted in the mother's womb.

ABORTION

It is important to recognize that abortion is not a battle between the unborn and the woman. The woman who has an abortion is like a trapped animal who gnaws its leg to escape. For a woman sometimes the only escape is to have an abortion. The woman who has an abortion feels lonely and afraid. Most of the time she is following the advice of someone she loves and respects, the father of her child or her mother. However, a kind word instead of condemnation may lead to another alternative. Although the writer is pro-life, he does have empathy for a woman who has an abortion. Abortion is not the right solution. It is like saying two wrongs make a right. The first wrong was in conception. The second wrong was stopping a beating heart. It is known that a married woman may have an "unwanted" pregnancy but the fact remains that there was conception and the killing of the unborn child is not the proper response to the problem. This is not intended to be a chapter on abortion but it has become part of our society. It is important to mention it as part of the discussion on when life begins. It is clear that abortion stops a beating heart. The stance against abortion need not pit the child against the mother.

ABORTION OPTIONS

As stated earlier, abortion is likened to gnawing off of an animal's leg to escape a trap. Unlike the animal, a mother has other options. There is not enough information out there about other options. Crisis Pregnancy Centers do a tremendous job assisting those who come to them. Yet the news media does not carry the message of hope. The assistance from Pregnancy Centers including food, clothing, medical attention, and shelter seldom gets reported. Saving lives does not seem to carry as much weight with the new media as taking lives. When was the last time you read or heard about a life being saved versus life being taken?

We said earlier that we would discuss the fact that the medical profession is not immune from the law. Consider the fact that the law states that the medical profession will be cited in a birth certificate and a death certificate. In between the law states that a physician will exercise reasonable and proper care in treating a patient. So the law affects a physician's action from birth through death of an individual. In most states it is a crime for a doctor to assist someone who wants to take their own life. We could go on with other examples of how the law impacts the medical community but the point is that actions taken by a physician and the staff are affected by laws. Thus even though the two do not agree on when life begins, law nevertheless impacts the medical community.

4

Is There a Trinity?

One conversation on this issue showed that the person was unsure about his understanding on the issue. He was truly searching for God but was uncertain about the God he was to obey. Are there three gods or is it three gods who represent one God? Of course there is a denomination that assured him there is no trinity. Another denomination assured him that there is. Who to believe? The Bible does not use the word trinity therefore what is all this talk about a trinity? Let's examine the concept.

TRINITY NOT FOUND

It is true that the Bible does not use the term. Try the word search on your computer and all you will find are non-Bible references to the word. Look for it in your concordance and come up with a disappointment. Look in the dictionary. No reference to the Bible. When the conversation took place we examined several sources but could not come up with a good description other than to say that it is embraced in a concept stated in the Bible. Conceptually there is no problem

accepting the principle that a trinity could be possible. In fact many
entities can reside in one place at the same time.

MANY EQUAL ONE

Take a father for instance. He can be a brother, uncle, cousin, hus-
band, employee, etc., all at the same time and yet he is one. Another
instance is that we live in a body, have a soul, and have a spirit. This
may not satisfy the concept of Father, Son, and Holy Ghost.
However it satisfies the requirement that more than one title can
apply to a single entity. Also we may consider the thought that there
are many members in one body. The conversation concluded that
these were functions and therefore did not qualify to establish the
trinity under discussion.

THE EGG

Then another item was explored that might more closely approximate
the kind of trinity that comes to mind when we hear that word. This is
the use of the egg analogy. According to this thought when one talks
about an egg there are three distinct components which are all parts of
the one egg. First there is the shell. Without a shell the egg could not
exist. Then there is the egg white and finally there is the yoke. These
three components make up the egg. There cannot be one without the
other. Thus, there is a trinity in the egg. Similarly when one talks about
the Father, Son, and Holy Ghost one can be talking about the entity of
God. Let's look at some Biblical references to see if we can make a case.
Bible references are used to both establish that there is a trinity and that
there is not a trinity. Which is correct? Let's see what we find.

ONE LORD

First of all we can go to Deuteronomy 6:4 which states that the Lord
our God is one Lord. This makes a case for a single entity. However
when looking at John 10:30 we find that Jesus claims that He and the
Father are one. This leads us to conclude that God has at least two

parts. This would leave us with two parts of an egg. Since an egg consists of three entities can we make the case that God also consists of three entities? So far we have talked about two entities. Does the Bible talk about a third entity? John records in I John 5:7 that three bear record in heaven and that these three are one. The entities he talks about are the Father, the Word, and the Holy Ghost. There is no mention of Jesus in this passage. However in John 1:1 he says that in the beginning was the Word, and the Word was with God, and the Word was God. Therefore one can conclude that the Word spoken of here is God. Jesus contends that He and God are one. Therefore, in the mention of those three entities in I John 5:7 one can equate Jesus with the Word. Know that the Word became flesh or so we are to believe if we believe John chapter 1 verse 14 which says in part that the Word was made flesh, and dwelt among us. Who else but Jesus did he have in mind when he says, "and dwelt among us?" It is very clear that the Word spoken of in John 1 verse 1 is referring to Jesus. Thus when we read in Matthew 28:19 about baptizing in the name of the Father, the Son, and the Holy Ghost, we are talking about baptizing in the name of one God. There is disagreement among some as to which name should be used in baptism.

BAPTISM

Some say that we should baptize in the name of Jesus only because the new testament stresses that name. Although this chapter does not deal with baptism, we will digress a bit and talk about being baptized in the name of Jesus only. Suffice it to say that the name of Jesus invokes the name of the Father, the Son, and the Holy Ghost. Just like when saying egg invokes the name of the shell, yoke and egg white. Still, the Bible does not command us to baptize in the name of Jesus. It commands us to baptize in the name of the Father, the Son, and the Holy Spirit. Another topic that is mentioned in connection with baptism is its symbolism of the death and rising from the dead, experienced by Christ. Total immersion makes a public portrayal of acceptance of that event. Other forms of baptism do not encompass portrayal of those events. Let's examine baptism a little further. What is baptism? First of all according to Acts 8:36 it takes water. Then when we read verses 38 and 39 we conclude that it means going down into and coming up out of the water. And as portrayed in Colossians 2:12 it is a picture of a death, burial and resurrection. Does anything besides total immersion make such a picture?

TRINITY

Back to the subject of trinity. Earlier it was said that there were three entities or functions of God. Three equals trinity. Like a father can be a son, brother, uncle, etc., it can be said that God is the Father, the Son and the Holy Ghost. This contention does not appear in the book as something new. The Bible addresses the subject. Now are the three one? There is one if one is to believe the Bible. It was stated earlier that the Bible would be relied on as the basic document to get to the truth. Other documents may be good but only the Bible is given by the inspiration of God. That is the way II Timothy 3:16 comes across when it states that all scripture is given by the inspiration of God. I John 5:7 has already been cited saying that the three are one. This and other verses make it possible that the Bible makes a strong case for a trinity. The word trinity is not mentioned but the concept is clearly there.

FALSE DOCTRINE

Thus one can believe that those denominations which are teaching that there is no trinity are teaching a false doctrine. The Bible tells us to avoid those who teach a false doctrine. Those who teach a false doctrine also teach a false Christ. Matthews 7:15 tells us to beware of false prophets. This brings us to another question that was mentioned when discussing the trinity. Who is a false prophet? II Corinthians 11:4 leads one to believe that anyone who preaches another gospel can be labeled a false prophet. Therefore as Paul advised, check everything against the scriptures. This means that one is to study and be knowledgeable about what is in the Bible. It is true that we need teachers but the final word is the Bible. God not only gives us teachers but He also gave us His Word. We are to be washed with His Word. How does one get washed in the Word? The way to be immersed in His Word is to study His Word. That way one will not be swayed by false doctrines. One thing difficult about false doctrines is that they quote the scriptures to make their point. However, they are using only that part of scripture that supports their point of view. That is why it is important to study all of the scriptures that have a bearing on a particular issue.

FALSE TEACHERS

One cannot be too careful. Usually false teachers tickle our ears with sweet sounding scriptures. The scriptures they cite tend to relieve us of any responsibility and "be happy" because God is in control and he loves us. He would never hurt us. Any deviation from false prophets is considered to be in error. Thus according to false prophets anyone who believes in the trinity is in error. There is no doubt that the concept of the trinity has a sound basis even though the word is not mentioned in the Bible.

SODOM AND GOMORRAH

I'm going to deviate from the trinity because in that conversation there was a contention that God would never do anything to harm us. If this is the case, I wonder what He meant when He told Moses to put his hand into his bosom and when he took it out it was leprous (Exodus 4:6). Or when He sent locusts to Egypt? Again what did He mean in Exodus 15:26 when He told the Israelites that if they harkened to the voice of Lord, He would put none of these diseases upon them, which he had brought upon the Egyptians? Does this mean that God hurt the Egyptians by putting diseases on them? Some say that God allowed rather than put these diseases on the Egyptians. This may be so but I have not found any translations that so state. I know that people contend that a God of love cannot cause something bad to happen to someone. How about Sodom and Gomorrah? Did the loving God send fire to those cities? Was anyone burned or hurt in those cities? Even though God is merciful, long suffering, and gracious, He does reach the point where He says enough is enough. Hebrews 9:27 says, "And as it is appointed unto man once to die, but after this the judgment:" And then we can follow up with Jude 15 which reads, "To execute judgment upon all, and to convince all that are ungodly among them of all their ungodly deeds which they have ungodly committed, and all their harsh *speeches* which sinners have spoken against him." Then there is the judgment day. Many will hear "well done my good and faithful servant." Others will hear "away from me, I never knew you." Thus even though He is a loving God, **we** have to account for our actions.

One of our actions is believing that there is a trinity. We can also believe that there is not a trinity. That places us in a position of hearing "away from me, I never knew you." In that case who is to blame, the Lord or us? Remember, we are responsible for our actions. Do we believe His Word or the word of men? Some say if the word is not used in the Bible then the concept cannot be accepted. Thus according to some, the lifestyle of some is acceptable because the Bible does not mention certain lifestyles per se. This is dangerous ground not only for non-Biblical lifestyles but for not accepting the concept of God being a trinity and being sovereign.

5

COMMENTS ON THE GREAT TRIBULATION

Unlike the word trinity, the word tribulation does appear in the Bible. The concept is there and has caused some to conclude that people will experience a pre-tribulation period. These people conclude that Christians will not go through the tribulation. Some conclude that Christians will go through the tribulation while others contend they will emerge after the tribulation. This chapter will not address that issue. Instead it will address the issue whether there is a tribulation or not. To distinguish between a personal tribulation and the one under discussion we will refer to this one as the great tribulation.

TRIBULATION

To begin with, the dictionary does not address the issue under discussion. Instead it deals with the individual suffering. It is true that tribulation involves suffering. However the concept we are dealing with in this chapter involves whether or not there is such a thing as a great tribulation in the end times. People have been talking about the end time for a long time. One thing is certain, each day that passes brings us closer to that unknown day. That unknown day will bring both joy and suffering. This chapter deals with whether or not there will be a tribulation when Jesus returns.

JESUS WILL RETURN

There is a promise that Jesus will return. No one but the Father knows when that day will be. There will be certain signs as we approach that day. Some of these signs are spelled out in II Timothy 3:2 through 6 which talks about doing bad things. Some of these same conditions have been noted since ancient times. There have always been people who are boastful, proud, disobedient to parents, etc. We are witnessing that some are not only disobedient to parents, they are also disobedient to God. Surely this sounds much like conditions in the United States today. In fact it looks like II Timothy 3:2 through 6 is talking about conditions we are encountering today. Surely we are witnessing conditions fore-told for the last days. We are approaching the day of judgment. As noted else-where some will hear the words "well done my good and faithful servant," others will hear "away from me, I never knew you." For as it says in Proverbs 20:27, "The spirit of man is the candle of the Lord, searching the inward parts of the belly." He will judge based upon what is in the heart, not on the outward appearance. There is no question but that the day of the Lord will come as a thief in the night. It will be too late to change conditions of the heart at that time. Some will rejoice because of the judgment, others will not. For some there will be crying and gnashing of the teeth. This is sad but true.

DAY OF RETURN

We are getting closer to the day when we will see the Son of man coming in a cloud with power and great glory. Beware of people who predict the exact day as no one but the Father knows when that day will come. All we know is that the signs are pointing to that day. Some are looking forward to that day, others don't care, and still others are fearing that day. However, we are assured that such a day is coming. Some of us may live to see that day. Most of us have heard about that day. That is the beginning of a great tribulation. For sure there will be much weeping and gnashing of the teeth for some as well as great joy for others.

TWINKLING OF AN EYE

When I say that some are looking forward to that day I am talking about those who expect to be swept away and changed in a twinkling of an eye. Those remaining behind will surely experience suffering. Those people are going through the great tribulation. But will Christians go through that period or will they be taken up before that time? According to Luke 17:34 and 35 it is apparent that some will be taken and others left behind. Can we make a case that Christians will be taken and non-Christians left behind? Some people cite Matthew 24:37 to contend that the non-Christian will be taken as in the day of Noe (Noah). Be that as it may, at this time we cannot say who will be taken and who will be left. The important point that those scriptures want to emphasize is the fact that sinners and saints will both be in the world at the same time. More on this later.

CORRUPTION AND INCORRUPTION

Before we examine that concept, we must lay some groundwork. Let's back up and see what we can find. First of all if I Corinthians 15:50 which talks about corruption and incorruption is correct, and it must be if the Word is given by the inspiration of God, we find that flesh and blood cannot inherit the kingdom of God. Thus the changing in a twinkling of an eye must mean that people are changed from flesh and blood into something else that is not corrupt. Let's digress a little and see if the flesh is corrupt. We know that God sent His son in the likeness of sinful flesh. Therefore if the flesh is sinful, it must be corrupt. One would hardly think that something that is sinful could be righteous at the same time. Only the righteous will inherit the kingdom.

CHRISTIAN AND NON-CHRISTIAN

Which brings us back to looking at the Christian and the non-Christian. Does it seem possible that the non-Christian will inherit the kingdom? Is the Bible a love letter to the Christian and the non-Christian? It looks like the non-Christian shall go away into everlasting punishment. This appears to be, unlike Noah's time, those who are left behind and do not repent during the great tribulation. They take the mark of the beast. Those who were taken are to be changed into something incorruptible. That something incorruptible is not flesh and blood.

Having said that some will be taken and others left behind one can conclude that the non-Christian who does not repent is the one left behind. Left behind to endure all of the great tribulation. We still have not established that there is a great tribulation and when that time will be. For this we will look in the Old Testament as well as the New Testament. Deuteronomy 4:30 leads us to believe that one can experience a tribulation. But even in tribulation God will not forsake those going through the great tribulation. John 16:33 tells us that in the world ye shall have tribulation.

Some contend that tribulation can be associated with old age because the elderly are generally sick. There seems to be an exception because many old folks are in good health. The great tribulation under discussion is universal and affects the young and old alike. Thus the tribulation we are talking about here comes at the end time. It must be remembered that time is a man-made measurement and that to God the passage of time is much different than it is to man. Thus we are talking about man's end time and not God's end time. He is eternal. Man's spirit is eternal but life on this earth is measured in time and thus there is an end time for mankind. Is the end time different for the Christian and the non-Christian?

CHRISTIAN AND BELIEVER

First we must clarify the difference between Christian and non-Christian versus believer and nonbeliever. The reason the term Christian is used instead of believer is that the term believer can apply to those who believe on something other than the gospel of Jesus Christ. The term Christian is applied to those who are followers of Christ. This term leaves out those who believe in another god. There is quite a distinction when the word God is capitalized and when it is spelled with a lowercase "g". The uppercase is used whenever the term applies to the God of Abraham and Jacob and to the God that Christians worship. The lowercase "g" is used when referring to the god or gods of non-Christian followers.

END TIME

Back to the relationship between the great tribulation and the end time. How do we know the end time has not come when we see so many signs? For one thing, the sun has not been darkened as mentioned in Mark 13:24. For another, we have not seen the sheep and the lion together. Nor have we witnessed the whole creation groaning. We are seeing people groaning and parts of the earth groaning but the whole creation is not groaning. The main purpose in discussing this subject is repentance rather than rejection. The establishment and maintenance of a right relationship with the Lord makes one understand and not fear the great tribulation. On the other hand Romans 2:9 tells us of tribulation and anguish upon every soul of man that doeth evil. A right relationship with God will ensure that we do not do evil. Thus, we do not have to fear the great tribulation at the end time. Whether dead or living we will be aware of the return of Jesus. Dead in this sentence refers to physical death rather than dead because of separation from God.

JUSTIFIED BY BLOOD

Those who are dead because of separation from God will experience the great tribulation. Those who have been justified by the blood of

Jesus shall be saved from his wrath or so we are led to believe in Romans 5:9 which so states. Earlier it was said that flesh and blood will not inherit the kingdom of God. That is true but being justified by his blood does not mean that blood will inherit such kingdom. The subject of blood sacrifice is too complex to address in this chapter. Suffice it to say that those who are justified by the blood of Jesus will not go through the great tribulation. This does not mean that they will not face a personal tribulation during the life on earth because of persecution for His name. In fact Christians will endure persecution because they believe in Christ. However, this does not compare with the great tribulation. But even if it did, it was prophesied in II Chronicles 20:9 that Christians would stand when evil cometh upon them and Romans 8:35 through 39 implies nothing will separate them from the love of Christ.

MARK OF THE BEAST

There will be those who go through the great tribulation and come out on the other side still clinging to a new found belief in God and have washed their robes and made them white in the blood of the Lamb. This was revealed to John as he stated in Revelation 7:14. So when it is said that Christians will not experience the great tribulation the statement has to be modified to exclude those who came to Christ during the great tribulation. There will be those who during that time do not take the mark of the beast and emerge victorious through Christ. This gives credence to those who contend that Christians will go through the great tribulation. But don't be caught up in the debate about pre-tribulation, tribulation, post-tribulation status of Christians. Instead concentrate in developing and maintaining a right relationship with the Lord at this time. The tribulation events will take care of themselves. We don't have to be worried about the event.

THOUSAND YEAR REIGN

It is mentioned here to say that such an event will take place. There will be a rule on this earth by God and his people. Some people are looking forward to that time. Others are concerned that the devil will be loosed for a season after the thousand years and will deceive many. The thousand year reign and reigning forever and ever were discussed in connection with the great tribulation but emphasis is on the great tribulation. It was felt that the great tribulation and what is known as the end time will occur simultaneously. The reasoning for this is found throughout the New Testament. Suffice it here to say that those who were seeking God wanted assurance of salvation.

6

COMMENTS ABOUT HEAVEN AND HELL

Many people are convinced that there is a heaven but no hell. Some debate the issue of what constitutes hell. In this chapter we will examine what people have to say about the subject as well as what the Bible teaches. The thought in the first sentence is like saying there is a positive but no negative. Such a condition is not found in nature. Is it possible for such a condition to exist in the spiritual world? This is an interesting concept. After all the spiritual world is not governed by the natural world.

HEAVEN

First to the subject of heaven. Is there such a place? Where is it? What is it like? How big is it? As mentioned in the opening sentence of this chapter, many people believe there is such a place. What does the Bible say about it? First of all Psalms 14:2 says that the Lord looked down from heaven. This tells us two things. First, there is a heaven from which the Lord looked at us. Second, heaven is somewhere other than down. Then there is Psalms 102:19 which says that the Lord looked down and beheld the earth. Thus we conclude that heaven is somewhere up or so we are led to believe in Psalms 103:11 which says the heaven is high above the earth. Some people contend that heaven is on earth and they go so far as to say that hell is here also.

Of course there are many more verses that talk about heaven. We can't quote all of them here. That is not the purpose of this chapter. Suffice it to say that the Bible says there is a heaven. Where is it? It has already been established that it is not on earth. Both Isaiah 66:1 and Acts 7:44 contend that heaven is the Lord's home and the earth is his footstool. This still doesn't tell us where heaven is located. We know that John was told to write certain things about heaven because of the revelation he had. He even saw an angel come down from heaven. This still does not tell us where heaven is located other than somewhere above. We have to look above to see heaven.

We know that in the beginning God created the heaven but we don't know where. We know he called the firmament heaven. Perhaps we need to look for heaven in the firmament. Just what or where is the firmament? We know that the firmament is not the earth. We know from Genesis 1:20 that birds fly above the earth in the open firmament of heaven. From this we conclude that the firmament is around the earth. We refer to this area as space. We talk about near space and outer space. Thus we conclude that heaven is larger than the earth. In fact heaven is large enough for everyone to fit into. Imagine, if everyone that ever lived was alive today, there certainly wouldn't be room for all on earth. But heaven is larger and certainly takes in more people than earth. But no place will be found in heaven for those deceived by the devil.

THE FIRMAMENT

So far we have concluded that heaven is not on earth. It is in the firmament but what is it like? According to Matthew 25:14 the kingdom of heaven is as a man traveling into a far country. This doesn't tell us much so we have to look elsewhere. Matthew 5:16 tells us to glorify our Father who is in heaven. In another place the Bible says that he resides in our heart and that our body is His temple. Is this a contradiction or is it possible for He to be in many places at the same time? Think of it. He is in your heart and mine. This means that indeed He can be in more than one place at the same time. It then makes sense that He can occupy heaven as His throne while at the same time living in our bodies. Moving on to seek where heaven might be. We have already established that it is not on earth. We have also established that it is in the firmament surrounding the earth. Thus from our perspective we can say that it is up. We know from Matthew 3:17 that a voice came from heaven. In the verse before that we see that Jesus saw the Spirit of God descending like a dove. This leads us to believe that indeed heaven is somewhere up as nothing descends from below. Also the up is from any point on earth as it has been stated that the firmament surrounds the earth.

HELL

This raises an interesting point as we have been led to believe that hell is somewhere. Does this down mean that hell is somewhere down in the earth? Let's begin by addressing the term hell before we try to establish its location. As was stated earlier, there are many who contend there is no hell. Still others contend that we live in our own hell here on earth and that it doesn't make sense that we should be punished throughout eternity for wrongs committed for a short time on earth. It is ironic that the same people who believe we will not be punished for eternity believe that heaven is for eternity and those who go to heaven will enjoy eternal rewards. Again this is like saying there can be a positive without a negative. Or since positives attract negatives, the negatives disappear. The disappearance theory cannot be substantiated. Thus we can conclude that if there is a heaven there is a hell.

WHERE IS HELL?

We know from Luke 10:19 that Jesus saw Satan fall from heaven fast as lightning. Where did Satan go when he fell from heaven? We know he went down somewhere. Thus, the term down can imply any place other than heaven. This makes the case for hell being somewhere besides down in the earth. However, we know that Jesus went down to hell after the crucifixion. He was buried in the ground thus giving some the impression that hell must be down in earth. However, when one looks at the case of the rich man and the beggar we see that the rich man was looking far off. Again one can make the case that since the rich man was buried then hell must be in the ground. Then again upon reading Luke 16:23 we don't know where he was in torment. Saying hell can be compared to saying America. There are 50 states in America. One can get more specific by naming a state in America. One can get even more specific by naming a city. To get more specific one can name the street and even get down to the address. Similarly when one says "hell" one is not getting down to a specific address but rather a place distinguished from "heaven." Thus we don't know the specific address where the rich man was in torment. Hell is a very big place. It can never be filled up. This makes a good case for it not to be limited by the confines of the earth.

FIRE AND BRIMSTONE

On the other hand, some people have imagined it to be a place of fire and brimstone. As was brought out in the conversation, there is a great temperature as we go deep into the earth. Science confirms this. However, the lake of fire burning with brimstone is somewhere other than the center of the earth. The molten lava that is deep within the earth makes a convenient imagination for the lake of fire. However, Revelation 20:14 makes it clear that hell was cast into the lake of fire. Thus, hell and the lake of fire are not the same thing. Our discussion was on hell rather than the lake of fire. Originally when Satan was cast down did he go to hell or to the lake of fire? We know that later he roamed the earth and presented Eve with the opportunity to sin. First he questioned God's word. Then he convinced Eve that she could be like God and know good and evil. And finally he convinced Adam to give him the earth over which he had dominion. He is a deceiver all right. Even today he keeps on deceiving people. This means he is not in hell at this time.

TORMENT

Conversations led to the conclusion that hell is somewhere other than where tradition has led some to believe it is. There is no satan dressed up in a red suit with two horns and a place burning with fire and brimstone. Instead hell is a place of torment. That torment may feel like fire but unlike normal fire, the object burning is not consumed. The torment goes on forever and ever. Ask the rich man who saw the beggar a far off. The torment spoken of in Luke 16:24 is in fact a flame. This leads us to conclude that there is a fire in hell. That duration in hell is more than just a short time is also confirmed in these verses in Luke. There is a great chasm between heaven and hell. The scripture doesn't say the beggar was in heaven. It says he was carried into Abraham's bosom. This brings up another interesting question. Where is Abraham's bosom?

ABRAHAM'S BOSOM

It may seem like we are getting off course but we are examining the concept of heaven and hell. First of all, we need to establish the whereabouts of Abraham. When he died physically, he was buried. We've heard of a number of heavens. Some people even talk about the 7th heaven. Where was Abraham at the time we are talking about? When we talk about being carried into Abraham's bosom, do we mean inside Abraham or are we referring to something like in Numbers 11:12 where a nursing father carries a child in his bosom? Perhaps we can look at Proverbs 19:24 where it says that a man hideth his hand in his bosom. The same principle can be applied to Luke 16:22. Thus we can conclude that being in Abraham's bosom is being with him, not in him. But in which heaven was Abraham? Some say he was in the third heaven, others say something else, but what does the Bible say?

REWARD AND PUNISHMENT

God is in heaven. Is Abraham? Does this mean that Abraham resides in our hearts as well as heaven? No, but we are Abraham's seed if we do the works of Abraham. Rather than asking if Abraham is in the 1st, 3rd, or 7th, heaven we should ask in what place besides hell is Abraham. Then clearly we conclude that indeed he is in heaven. Now heaven is a big place just like the United States. We don't know exactly in which state Abraham resides. All we know is that he is in heaven. With this in mind and the fact that the Bible mentions heaven 551 times and hell 54 times we conclude that there are places of eternal reward and eternal punishment. Having determined that there is a heaven how do we get there? According to John 3:7 we must be born again. And Matthew 18:3 tells us that we must be converted. Some kind of change must occur in us before we can go there. No change is required to go to eternal punishment. However we must get off the broad and wide road and follow Jesus. Sounds too hard? It is not for freeloaders! God wills that all mankind go to heaven but He knows that only a few will make it. He leaves that up to us. A little organ can speak life or death. We control that organ. We have the option of choosing life or death. Choose life. Live and go to heaven.

BIBLICAL HELL

This brings us to some thoughts about hell. There are those who claim that it is somewhere down in the earth and that it smells of burning brimstone. Others contend that it is on the surface of the earth and that people live their own heaven and hell. Still others contend that hell is a place of torment and do not assign it a location. This latter group has a closer understanding of what the Bible is talking about when it mentions hell. They are correct when they agree with Psalms 9:17 which states that the wicked shall be turned into hell as well as the nations that forget God. Then there are other admonitions for those who do not keep God's commandments. Of course He does not expect perfection but He does expect people not to act contrary to His Word.

Thus with the Bible as an authority we conclude that there is indeed a hell and that people will go there. Jesus went there but did not remain there. Some contend that since He got out that they will also get out. This theory fits in nicely with the belief that they will not be tormented for eternity because of sins committed during their brief journey through earth. This sounds possible, but is it true? How long was the rich man described in Luke 16:23 tormented? Then consider the revelation of John as in Revelation 1:18. Jesus says that He liveth and was dead. He holds the keys of hell and of death. From this we know He is alive and according to Acts 2:31 His soul was **not** left in hell. There is nothing in the scriptures to support the theory that He was left in hell. But there is a clear statement in Matthew 10:28 that we are to fear him which is able to destroy both soul and body in hell. Satan works on the body while mankind inhabits the earth and then torments the soul while in hell. Do not take Satan's attack personally, he only wants to prove the Word wrong. However, we are the ones who make it possible to be deceived by not studying to show ourselves approved of God.

FATHER

It is time to leave this conversation and go on to the one of who should be called father on earth. There are both a biological father and a spiritual father. Should we refer to someone else as father here on earth? Read the next chapter for a discussion on that.

.

7

WHOM SHALL WE CALL FATHER?

There is no question that all individuals have a biological father. We refer to that biological entity as father. Should we call anyone else father? How about our spiritual father? Do we have a spiritual father? What did Jesus tell Nicodemus? Who is your father when you are born again? Then Hebrews 12:9 talks about fleshly fathers and a spiritual Father.

BIOLOGICAL BIRTH

First we will look at the natural birth and the person whom we call father. There are many biology books which go into detail about conception, growth within the womb, and delivery on birth. This book will not cover those details. Instead we will concentrate on the aspect of whom we shall call father. As stated before, we have an earthly father whom we have no problem calling "father."

SPIRITUAL BIRTH

Having established that we have a biological father let us look at the possibility of having a spiritual Father. As asked earlier, who is the Father when one is born again? That birth unlike the physical birth involves someone who is already born of the flesh. It is clear from scripture that one born of the flesh is sinful. To wash away this sin so as to enter into the kingdom of God one must be born again. Since it is not possible for one to enter the mother's womb and be born again there must be another way. Unlike the physical birth the spiritual birth is not marked by physical delivery. There is a delivery that takes place but like the unseen wind that goes where one cannot tell, or where it comes from. This then seems like an out of body experience. But is it like the term commonly used? We know that that which is born of the flesh is flesh, and that which is born of the Spirit is spirit. We know that corruption cannot enter heaven and the flesh is corrupt.

UPPER CASE AND LOWER CASE LETTERS

Let's digress a little and examine the uppercase S in spirit and the lowercase s. The principle stated here applies to all uppercase and lowercase letters used in the Bible but we will only address the letter s in this case. It has generally been understood that when we see the word spirit with a capital S it refers to the Holy Ghost. The lowercase s refers to the spirit of man. Thus in John 3:6 it is clear that the rebirth is born of the Holy Ghost leaving the spirit of man dwelling in man. However, the spirit of man is now subject to the Spirit of God. I thought the spirit of man was subject to the Holy Ghost and not God. The Holy Ghost is part of the Godhead. Thus, being subject to the Holy Ghost is being subject to God. The flesh is subject to God so what is the big deal if the spirit is now subject to the Spirit? Nicodemus wondered how these things can be. Jesus wondered how Nicodemus could be a master of Israel and not know these things. Similarly one who is born again knows that the beginning of knowledge is fear of the Lord. If one cannot understand earthly things it is difficult to understand heavenly things?

BORN AGAIN

This matter of being born again is a heavenly thing. Thus someone who is not born again cannot see the kingdom of God. Based on these conversations and other input I've concluded that men today find themselves much in the position that Nicodemus was in when he encountered Jesus. There is so much earthly information that men are perplexed when they hear about Jesus. They ask how can these things be? It is as though they should know as much about life as Jesus. They know they have a fleshly father; now if they are born again, they must have another father and mother. The subject of father and mother are not mentioned in connection with the new birth. This chapter deals with the subject of who should be called father. We will leave the subject of motherhood to John 3:12 which states that if we don't believe earthly things how are we to believe heavenly things. The rest of the chapter emphasizes the role of the Father and so we will stick with examining the concept of who is our father. We have already established that we have an earthly father. Surely there is no question or confusion about referring to him as father. The question we are examining is, who if anyone else can we refer to as father?

FATHER

Some denominations refer to the leader of a congregation as father. After all he is the head of the local congregation and it is only natural to look at the head of something as father. This raises an interesting question. Is there anyplace in the scripture that sanctions calling the head of an organization father? A word search came up with Psalms 89:26 where David acknowledges God as the Father and earlier in Psalms 68:5 we see that He is a Father to the fatherless. There are other scriptures that confirm that God is our Father. Not only that, He is a jealous God. Jesus says in Matthew 23:9, call no man on earth your father. Does this include your biological father? It is very clear that

Jesus was referring to the heavenly Father in Matthew and not to the biological father. Thus the conclusion is clear that you are to call no man your father upon the earth: for one is your Father, which is in heaven. Where does this leave us when we want to show respect to the head of a congregation or the head of a denomination? According to Ephesians 4:11 He did give us pastors. Did He give us Fathers? We certainly have a biological father. Who else should we call father? According to the Bible we have a heavenly Father if we are born again. Thus, in addition to the biological father we can call God our Father. In fact, when Jesus taught the disciples to pray one of the things He urged then to acknowledge was "our Father which art in heaven." (Matthew 6:9) This leaves us with the conclusion that we should only refer to these two entities as father and no one else.

GOD

We can show respect for the head of a congregation or denomination by addressing them by some title other than father. In fact we are to be in submission to Godly leaders because He has blessed us by ordaining church government. However, all authority (civil and church) comes from God. In this country it looks like we elect civic leaders. However, the final or official appointment comes from God. We get the kind of government we deserve. Some people take issue with that theory however, they don't have another good explanation for the kind of government we get. Our character is reflected in our government. You may say, "not me, I didn't vote for so and so." This government does not reflect my character. In reading from Jeremiah and Daniel one can conclude that we are all in the same boat. Thus it is our government and a reflection of our character even if we voted differently, or didn't vote at all, for the government we have. This gets us somewhat off the subject of whom we should call father. But the point here is that we don't refer to someone as father just because they are lifted up by God. He lifts some up and brings some down according to His will. We are not to refer to any of these lifted up men as father. That title is reserved for God and our biological father. Thus we go back to Matthew 23:9 and confirm that your Father is in heaven. However, we are free moral agents but we ought to obey God rather than man if we believe Acts 5:29. Jesus plainly tells us that brethren are to refer to God as Father.

SECOND LOOK AT MALE AND FEMALE

That brings us again to a side issue as to whether God is male or female. We have already addressed this issue but it bears a second look. Some say He is neither because He is a Spirit. After all, John 4:24 says he is a Spirit. This does not address the matter whether He is male or female. However, is it logical to call a female father? There are several scriptures that refer to a goddess. However, all these scriptures refer to goddesses in a negative way. There are many scriptures that lend support to the theory that God is a male. Some say that the Bible is biased and calls Him a male because it was written by men. That is true but if we believe II Timothy 3:16 all scripture is given be the inspiration of God. God is the entity that inspired the Word to use the male gender when referring to God. Are we to question the inspiration given by God? Are humans more knowledgeable than God? Is the Bible inerrant? If the answer to these questions is yes then what is the big problem in calling the Father a he? Can we pick and choose which parts are inerrant? To be consistent we have to believe either all of it or none of it. I think the case is made to believe all of it.

LOVE

Thus we arrive at the conclusion that we ought to be careful whom we call father here on earth. A father loves his children. Most leaders of a congregation can be said to love the congregation as a father loves his children. Yet one can distinguish between the kind of love of a father for his children and the love of a church leader for the flock. Like a judge said about pornography, I don't know how to define it but I know it when I see it. The same can be said of love of a father for his children and a church leader's love for the congregation. Thus recognizing this kind of love it does not make sense for members of congregation to call a church leader a father. At least that was the conclusion reached in this conversation. It is a good conclusion.

ERROR

At the risk of beating a dead horse to death it is necessary to pursue this subject a little further. Earlier it was said that the Bible says to call no man on earth Father. It is very clear then that denominations which call a dignitary of a church a father are in error. Another error which is committed is to call someone Reverend. That as a title of respect for a man is not in accordance with its use in the Bible. In Psalms 111:9 that title refers to the holy one which is God. Men who are saints and revered are not worthy of the title "Reverend." Even Haman though he was revered was not given the title of Reverend. That title seems to be reserved for the one who is holy and reverenced is His name. At first it might seem that it is OK to call someone on earth who is revered "Reverend." However, there is no scriptural basis for doing such. Thus the title Father and Reverend apply only to God and not to mortals.

Enough said on that subject. It is time to move on to something else. Needless to say, the conversations on this subject were genuine as there was a real thirst for searching for God. As was stated before, the Word and not man's opinion is considered the final authority. Thus regardless of what men think, that thought is all right so long as the thinking lines up with the Word.

REVEREND

As a bonus we see that the title of Reverend like the title Father refers only to God and not to man. This was the conclusion reached after several conversations and looking at the word given by the inspiration of God.

8

WHY ARE THERE MANY DENOMINATIONS IN CHRISTIANITY?

This seems to be a good question considering the fact that many so-called religions are not split like Christianity. Another question that was posed during the conversations was which was the "true" or best denomination in Christianity. This is answered when the broader question of many denominations in Christianity is explored. It became apparent that one had to consider the individual's relationship to Christ rather than his relationship to a particular denomination. With this said let's start looking at denominations and individuals.

DENOMINATIONS

All Christian denominations that teach that Jesus is the Son of God have a foundation based on scripture. God probably revealed something to the leader of a congregation. The leader in turn disclosed to the congregation what God had said to him. Many people thought that was the way to do things and so a new denomination was formed. It turned out to be a good thing. However, it soon was concluded that this formula leads to the "true church" and that those who did not follow these beliefs were doing something not of God. God would not be put in a box by man so he revealed something else to another individual. This revelation led to the formation of another denomination. The process of concluding that this is the "true church" continues in many denominations. Thus, we have many denominations in Christianity. But most denominations have some universal beliefs about Christianity. For example, all believe in the creator. Thus all acknowledge Genesis and the fact that there is a God. All agree that Jesus is the Son of God. All agree that the Bible was given by the inspiration of God. All believe that salvation is from God and that the only way we can come to Him is through His son Jesus. All teach about sin, salvation, heaven, hell, good and evil. Thus we see that there is agreement on the major issues. There is much disagreement on minor issues. Do we want to major on the minor? People are sincere about their understanding of the minor issues. However, someone is sincerely wrong. Being right on these minor issues will not determine whether one gets to heaven or not. Likewise, being wrong about these minor issues will not keep one out of heaven.

UNITY IS NOT UNIFORMITY

With that in mind many of the conversationists concluded that they understood why there are many denominations in Christianity. It is hoped that you see where these thoughts are coming from. With this understanding it is easy to see that in this diversity there is unity. The kingdom of God places everyone in one big boat rather getting its character from a flotilla of small boats. When we focus on denominations, we see a bunch of little boats rather than recognizing diversity in one big boat. There are some movements which are encouraging us to concentrate on the big boat rather what appears to be a flotilla of many small boats. The movements recognize diversity while acknowledging that we are all in the same boat. Thus we see that unity does not mean uniformity. There can be much diversity, not division among the many Christian denominations. The outside world, and many in the Christian world, have focused on the boats of denomination rather than on the big boat of Christianity.

UNITED IN CHRIST

There has been a strong emphasis on looking at denominations as something being true belief and someone of another denomination being outside the will of God. There has been some movement towards unity in the ecumenical sense. But this seemed to be man's effort at spiritual unity. This is different from the movement of the Holy Spirit. We now see the many denominations as being united in Christ. The movement of the Holy Spirit indwells people of a religion considered by Protestants as being outside the will of God. There is quite a difference between individuals of that denomination and the official statements or beliefs of that church. Thus one needs to be careful in referring to the people and not the denomination. Many people believe in God, Jesus and many of the other "Protestant" understandings of Christianity. The church itself may proclaim certain things troublesome to Protestants but many people embrace the so called "Protestant" beliefs while acknowledging many of the denomination's doctrines. However, God looks at the heart and not at the outside appearance. Humans tend to look at the outside because they are not privileged to see the intents of the heart. As a man thinketh in his heart so is he. Thus, regardless of denomination, God looks at the heart. For that reason many who appear to man as being lost are actually saved.

LOST AND SAVED

This brings up another interesting aspect. Who are the lost and who are the saved? For a long time it was thought those of a certain denomination were saved while all others were lost. Is this true? Can a denomination save one? According to the Bible salvation is from God and not from a denomination. Salvation is available to all mankind but some of mankind scoff at the idea. Salvation is available through faith by grace. Only by the grace of God do we have salvation. A denomination can dispense mercy but not grace. Mercy and grace can be defined as what we said before: in mercy we get what we deserve, in grace we don't get what we deserve. We deserve to go to hell but we don't go there because of grace.

Does Christianity place all religions or denominations in the big boat? The first chapter made the case that there is only one way to come to God. Many religions are based on something other than acknowledging that Jesus is the Son of God. Many of their teachings are similar to Christian beliefs, however the fact that they don't acknowledge Jesus as the Son of God is quite a deviation from the Word of God. Their teaching contends that A=B and B=C. Therefore it would seem that A=C. However, further examination reveals that A was dead. Christianity, on the other hand, serves a living God. A religion or denomination which serves a dead god cannot have a Christian doctrine. Therefore it is a religion that tries to offers the salvation found in Christianity. This is not to say that Christianity will save you. It merely indicates that without Christianity one is walking in darkness and is lost.

GRACE

As implied earlier, grace is having unmerited favor. Only God can grant grace and that comes through faith, the belief that Jesus is the Son of God and repentance. Grace is there for the taking. It is free, however, it is conditional. Since mankind is a free agent, one can meet the conditions if one repents and has the faith to accept salvation. Such cannot come from religions that do not acknowledge Jesus as the Son of God. Thus, not all religions are in the big boat. Some are striving to get by as part of a flotilla. They contend that all rivers flow to the sea therefore it doesn't make any difference if one is in a small boat or riding the big boat. As was pointed out in the first chapter, the analogy is flawed in that it does not recognize the cycle involved in rivers returning to their source.

A deceptive description makes it look like the real thing when in fact it is contrary to the Word of God. There is only one way to come to the Father and that is to come through the Son. All other doctrines lead elsewhere. Therefore, only Christianity including its many denominations is on the right track. All other religions have signs of darkness, cause one to stumble and lose the way. Many religions cannot stand the light of truth.

UNITY IN DIVERSITY

This brings us back to the proposition that many Christian denominations reflect a divisiveness and therefore not a unity found in other religions. As pointed out earlier, there is unity in diversity. To look at it as division rather than diversity is to miss the mark. Sure there is diversity in Christianity but as pointed out earlier there is agreement on major issues. The disagreement is over minor issues. Besides all the agreement cited earlier all Christian denominations believe in Matthew 3:17 which says that Jesus is the Son of God. They also accept Matthew 1 and Luke 1 that Jesus was born of a virgin. There is also agreement that sin separates mankind from God and that man must repent if he wishes to be saved. The issue of repentance is found in Luke 13:3. The word perish in that passage means the opposite of being saved. All Christian denominations agree that without faith it is impossible to please Him. The subject of faith was touched on earlier in the chapter. There can be misguided faith such as is found in religions other than Christianity. The energy expended in having faith in false religions should be applied to faith in the true living God and His Word, not man's word. He gave us His Word by His inspiration. Many false religions try to use intellect to make their point. Man's intellect is like filthy rags compared to God's Word.

We could go on noting the agreement among Christian denominations but the case is that there is unity among the diversity. Not all so called "Christian activity" can be viewed in a favorable light. However, all Christian action which relies upon the teachings of Jesus is favorable.

9

DOES GOD INTERVENE
IN THE AFFAIRS OF MAN?

These, like other conversations, were interesting. They ranged all the way from those who contended that we were like clocks, God winds us up and sets us on earth with no further thought. Then there were those who contended that we had no choice since we were predestined to go to heaven or hell. One thing rang in every conversation, everyone was searching for God. They were all sincere. Some were sincerely wrong.

CLOCKWORK

Those who believed we were put on earth and then left alone contended that there were indications of these conditions. There was a strong belief that at the end there was neither a heaven nor hell. This subject was addressed in chapter six. However, let's stick to the subject of intervention. The thought that we were left alone also contended that prayer did not change things. We will cover prayer later in this chapter but for now let's go with those who believed man could not cry out to God and have the course of events changed. To back up such a belief they pointed out such things as bad things happening to Christians. It was contended that a loving God would watch out for his people and not permit bad things to happen to them. The subject of a loving God permitting bad things to happen and using that evil for his glory will be discussed later.

MAN CREATED

For now let's look at some of the reasons cited for believing that we are placed on the earth and that is the end of God's involvement with mankind. Of course such a belief acknowledged a creator and evolution since being created. This is not a discussion of evolution verses creation. However, it is interesting to note that such a belief states categorically that God creates man. After the creation there is no more communication between God and man. Such a theory holds that man controls the events during one's lifetime. Thus man is a free moral agent and there is no accountability or judgment. This makes it wonderful for those who do not want their actions to be judged. The responsibility and accountability is strictly their business and God has nothing to say about it. Oh, if this were only so. We will look at some scriptures to explore this thought further. Suffice it for now to say that God is concerned with the affairs of man but he does not direct man's every move.

FREE MORAL AGENTS

The thought that He directs our every move does not recognize the fact that we are free moral agents. Being free moral agents sounds much like the contention that God leaves us alone after He creates us. We will take a closer look at whether man is a loose cannon ball or a robot. If we are mere robots then it can be said that we are like puppets with God pulling our strings. Of course there is a difference between a robot and a puppet. However, the conversations seemed to classify the two about the same. Further discussion led to the conclusion that we are neither. If we are not a puppet or a robot, what are we? It was kind of hard to reconcile free moral agent with predestination. However, the conversations led to a clear distinction. There was no doubt that man was not like a machine. He is not programed to do certain things. However, the Father does will that **all** be saved. He knows that many will reject Him. He does not send people to hell. People make their own decision to go there. The sinner can go to heaven if he confesses his sin and repents. On the other hand, a self-righteous person can lose his "so called" salvation if he thinks he can sin because he has been righteous in the past. He too needs to repent. God wants all to repent and be saved. It is His will but not His mandate. He loves all mankind but all mankind does not love Him. Hebrews tells us to forget NOT His law; but let thine heart keep His commandments. He evaluates the heart and not the outward appearance. Hebrews 3:6 goes on to say that man is to acknowledge Him and He shall direct thy path. So much for being turned loose on earth. Scripture does not support such thinking

ROBOTS

Now for the thought that God controls our every move. Not only are we predestinated and our end is predetermined, but God controls our every move to make sure we stay on the preplanned route. We have no say in what we will do along the way. First of all let's look at what the Bible has to say about pre-destination. Romans 8:30 states in part that whom He did predestinate, them He also called: and whom He called, them He also justified. Ephesians 1:5 goes on to say that having pre-destinated us into the adoption of children by Jesus Christ to Himself, according to His will. The next verse continues with the praise of the glory of His grace, wherein He has made us accepted in the beloved. This fits in nicely with verses 11 and 12 which state in whom also we have obtained an inheritance, being predestinated according to the purpose of Him who worketh all things after the counsel of His own will: that we should be the praise of His glory, who first trusted in Christ.

But Romans 8:29 states for whom He did foreknow, He also did predestinate to be conformed to the *image* of His Son, that He might be
the firstborn among many brethren.

PREDESTINATION

Predestination is only applicable to being conformed to the *image* of
His Son and not to the events of this life and for all eternity. It is true
that God made man in His image. In fact Genesis 1:26 says "our"
image meaning that there is some kind of plurality in God. This was
addressed in chapter four. Equate foreknowledge with watching a
rerun. In watching a rerun one know what is going to happen next but
one does not predetermine or predestinate what will happen. God
views our actions as reruns because he knows the beginning and the
end. I say this because Proverbs 5:21 tells me that the ways of man
are before the eyes of the Lord. Does this mean that prayer cannot
change things along the way? Prayer can change the original scene so
that the "rerun" reflects the change. The Bible presents evidence of a
change along the way. We see in II Kings 20:6 where Hezekiah's life
on earth was lengthened. Then in verse ten the sun went back ten
degrees. In Joshua 10:12-13 there is an account of the sun standing
still for a full day. Incidentally when a computer model was run on
the position of the sun from now to way back, the computer cannot
account for the sun's location by a day and 10 minutes. Could this be
because they hadn't programmed Biblical writings into the equation?
Mathematically it is very easy to determine the sun's location day by day.
However such a calculation will be off by a day and 10 minutes if the calculation does not take into account the events described in Joshua and
Second Kings. Prayer does change things. God already knew that the
prayer was going to occur thus His original plan took that into account.
The "change" takes place in man's perception and not in God's overall
plan. This action reflects foreknowledge, not predetermination. After
all, man is a free moral agent.

CREATION OR EVOLUTION?

Perhaps we need to explain the free moral agent concept versus the so-called predestination thinking. To begin with, God created man. Those who contend that man evolved from some slimly ameba then have to conclude that everything else just happened through some kind of evolutionary process. It would lead one to conclude that man, stars, sun, earth and all the elements came into being by some evolutionary method. Instead it is easier to accept the fact that there is a master plan. The account of creation in Genesis gives us a firm foundation for believing that there is a master plan. In that plan we find God gave man the ability to obey Him or to be disobedient. Adam and Eve were given specific instructions that they could partake of every tree in the garden except one. That is like putting a bowl of candy before children and telling them not to eat any. That is a true test of obedience versus disobedience. It is not a case of putting temptation for the sake of temptation. It simply gives one a choice. Having the ability to choose makes one a free moral agent. There is no predestination to be disobedient. Having been disobedient man was given a chance to repent. God so loved the world that He sent His only begotten Son to make it clear that man had a choice. The matter of coming to Him was discussed in chapter one of this book. It is clear then that man's ability to choose makes him a free moral agent.

GOD INTERVENES

Back to the matter of whether God intervenes in the affairs of man. The writer witnessed an event that convinces him of God's intervention into the affairs of man. The writer, along with two others, was scheduled to make a presentation in a far off city beginning on a Monday. Everyone studied the airline schedules and concluded that the safest thing to do was to fly out on Sunday afternoon or evening to be ready for the Monday presentation. The writer wanted to attend Sunday night service in town. He saw that there was a flight leaving on

Monday morning that would get him there on time if everything went according to schedule. The writer than made a decision to attend Sunday night services and fly out on Monday. The two companions of the writer urged him not to take such a chance because that was cutting it too close for comfort. Nevertheless the writer was of the opinion that God was in control and that everything would be fine if he flew out on Monday morning. That having been settled the writer attended Sunday night services.

HEADWIND

The next morning the writer made sure that he got to the airport in plenty of time to catch the flight. The plane took off on time so I thought everything was going all right. About ten minutes into the flight the pilot came on the intercom and told us that we were bucking an 80-knot headwind and that the headwind would delay our arrival time by 15 minutes. There went my perfectly laid plan. Knowing that I had no control over the situation I did not panic. I just prayed and thanked God for a safe trip. It did not even occur to me to ask God to intervene on my behalf. Instead, subconsciously, I was like other humans and thought God was out of the picture. I don't know if others prayed that we get there on time. However, about 10 minutes later the pilot again came on the intercom and told us that the FAA had given him a new altitude and that instead of bucking a headwind and arriving late we would actually arrive 15 minutes early. Having flown a lot I knew that planes flying east to west flew at one altitude. Planes flying west to east are given another altitude. Similarly planes flying north to south were given a different altitude than planes flying south to north. All this is to avoid possible collisions. I was like the blind man in John 9:25 who did not know if the healing was from God or not. All he knew was that before he was blind but now he could see. I do not know what elevation the pilot was given by FAA or if it was from God. All I know is that before we were told we would be 15 minutes late and then we were told we would arrive 15 minutes early.

FIRST BAG

At the airport my bag was the first one to arrive. I thought this was good but there was still the matter of calling a taxi to take me to the place where I was to speak. (This was not a destination where taxis wait at the airport for arrivals.) As soon as I grabbed my luggage a man came up to me and asked me if I was so and so. He had a car waiting to take me to the place where I was to speak. I arrived there in plenty of time to relax, drink a beverage, eat something and mix with the crowd. I cite this incident not to show how righteous I am but rather to show that I am loved and why I believe that God intervenes in the affairs of man.

COINCIDENCE

Later when I was relaying this incident in one of my conversations, a fellow said that it was just a coincidence that my luggage was the first one. He said that as often as I flew it was just a matter of time before my luggage came in first. There would be times when my luggage was in the middle of the pile and times when my luggage would be the last to be taken off. There is no disputing that this could be the case. However, the probability that the plane would arrive early, that my luggage is the first on the turnstile, and that a man with a car would be waiting for me is no doubt too many coincidences to happen the same day. I am firmly convinced that there was divine intervention to make everything come together for me. You may think that all these were coincidences but I look at the situation as God intervening in the affairs of man. Certainly He was aware of my desire to assemble myself with other Christians and the predicament I would be in if the plane arrived late. I didn't even petition Him to get me out of my predicament. He knew my situation and He was totally in control.

GOD IS IN CONTROL

I may have left out some details but the point I was trying to illustrate is that things don't just happen. God intervenes in the affairs of man. Some may contend that all passengers benefitted from an early arrival and yet they had nothing to do with the situation. As I said before, I don't know if there were some who prayed for an early arrival and I benefitted from such prayer. However, that misses the point that God cares about everyone and that He, not man, is in control of human events. I doubt that coincidences can explain every situation. The law of averages would not support such claims. If it is not a coincidence, what is it? The word control isn't in the Bible. How do we know that God is in control? If He is not in control how can He restrain certain things? In Genesis 8:2 we see that God restrained the rain. In Genesis 7:4 it says He will cause it to rain. Cause and restraint are certainly elements of control. Like rapture and trinity, control does not appear in the Bible but the concept is certainly there.

10

LORD OF LORDS AND KING OF KINGS

In all the conversations it was evident that the topic was a search for God. Searching doesn't seem to be the right word. Even though the word "searching" is used in the title of the book, search implies looking for something or someone that is lost. God is not lost. Perhaps a more appropriate title would be Coming to God through Jesus Christ or simply saying Seeking after God, however, the impression I got from the conversationalists was that they were actually searching for God, and thus the title. Everyone seemed to be missing something. It was obvious that some were looking in the wrong places for answers. There was a genuine search for something to hang on to. They were looking for both evidence and logic. Seeds were sown that would help them turn away from false teachings. They knew inside that there was something better than what they had and were willing to expose themselves to God's Word. In accepting God's Word they were taking personal responsibility for serving Him. There was a sigh of relief when they realized that God was concerned about them. Their gods could not meet their needs. The biggest need was repentance. Another need was the recognition of the sovereignty of the Lord. Without repentance and the recognition of the sovereignty of God it is easy to be tossed to and fro by every wind of doctrine.

SEARCHING FOR FULFILLING

Although the conversations covered the waterfront, each individual seemed to stick to one topic. In fact, to be most effective, one needs to limit the discussion to the basics. One place to start is about the basic truths taught in the Bible. First of all where does the Bible come from? According to II Timothy 3:16 it is given by the inspiration of God. There is quite a difference between inspired by God and given by the inspiration of God. If the Word was inspired by God, instead of given by His inspiration, we would have trouble reconciling some of His teachings. However, it is easy to understand that man has a free will if we recognize the Word was given by the inspiration of God. This is not a subject to be discussed with new converts. Suffice it to quote the scripture and leave it at that. The point is that the Bible is authoritative because it was given by the inspiration of God. John 5:39 says to search the scriptures for they testify of Him. The Bible contains scientific statements which uninspired men could not have known at the time they wrote about such things. Medical science is now telling us what they told us in Leviticus 17:11 that life is in the blood. Science confirms Job 26:7 that He hangeth the earth upon nothing. Don't try to cover every scientific finding initially but move on to basic facts. Having established that the Bible is given by the inspiration of God we need to move on to the fact that there is a God. Genesis 1:1 and John 1:1 not only tell us that there is a God but that He is the Creator of all things. Does it make sense to think that one so mighty would create us and not reveal Himself to us? That He is a God of deliverance? He is love, (I John 4:8) yet He is angry with the wicked. (Psalms 7:11) That is because one can be angry and sin not. (Ephesians 4:20)

SIN AND SALVATION

There are other scriptures that support the fact that there is a God but we need to move on to teach people about sin and salvation, heaven and hell, good and evil, God and the devil, mercy and grace. Tell them about Jesus Christ, Son of God, (Matthew 3:17) born of a virgin, (Matthew 1 and Luke 1). Tell them that Jesus was crucified, buried and rose from the dead, ascended unto heaven and is coming again. Tell them to live according to teachings in the Bible. Tell them to read the entire Bible for we do not have the luxury of picking and choosing which scriptures we will obey. The Bible is not like a cafeteria where we take only the things that appeal to us. Do not be fooled by any man that preaches any gospel other than what is found in the Bible. Do not be confused by some religions that make part of the Bible a part of their doctrine. Matthew 26:41 says to watch and pray. To paraphrase Paul, check out what you hear against the scripture. Begin by checking out the scriptures mentioned or quoted in this book. Teach this principle to everyone in your witnessing. The Bible is the final authority. Yes, rely on the Holy Spirit for direction but be assured that what you hear from the Holy Spirit is **never** contrary to what is in the Bible. Knowing the word will keep one from being deceived. Study to show yourself approved.

BASICS

When you witness, stick to the basics, don't try to cover everything. There will be time to talk about such things as the rapture, trinity, the end times, etc. but the main thing is to point people towards God. You sow the seeds. He will take care of the harvest. Remember, you can't save anyone, only He can save someone. He will give them a new life, a rebirth if you will, or a born again experience. They may start with some complicated subject but lead them back to the basics. The complicated can only be understood after one has a firm foundation of the basics. Every house that will stand is built upon a firm foundation. Some people must be washed in the Word if they are not to be torn down by false doctrines that sound like the Word of God. There is only one King of kings and Lord of lords. (I Timothy 6:15 and Revelation 17:14) One interesting thing is that gods of religions other than Christianity are all dead. The God of Christianity is alive. Only a live God can keep promises. A dead god cannot deliver. Thus it is clear that there is only one King of kings and Lord of lords and that is the God recognized by Christianity. All others are fakes.

FAITH

A witness cannot answer every question. Some questions are foolishness. Some items have to be accepted by faith. Without faith it is impossible to please Him. What is faith? When you read Hebrews 11, the faith chapter, you discover some basic facts. First faith begins with a revelation from God. That faith comes from hearing and hearing by the Word of God, thus faith grows out of a relationship with God. Faith is **acting** on what you believe. Obviously there is a great difference between faith and presumption. Faith grows when what one is doing is based solidly on the Word of God. Faith will give one joy and peace. The things you do will glorify God. One has to be willing to wait for God to take action. Abraham and Sarah found out the hard way that God wanted them to be "dead" to conceiving children so they could not take credit for the event. One mark of the maturing Christian is the development of stronger faith. Faith means trusting the King of kings, Lord of lords. One cannot develop that trust unless one gets to know God. The relationship will be such that all of one's actions will be pleasing to the Father.

WORKS

This brings us to the point of saying that faith without works is dead. There are some people who become so heavenly minded that they are no earthly good. The works that one does are not to earn brownie points. They are simply the results of having faith. That faith comes from hearing the Word of God. This is where your witnessing comes in. After telling people about the King of kings and Lord of lords encourage your listeners to assemble themselves with other Christians. In other words, encourage them to go to church. Your witnessing is only the beginning. The thing is to develop a hunger for the Word of truth.

It is hoped that the recording of my conversations will be of some benefit to you and your witnessing. Surely you have had similar conversations. Have you ever considered using such information to help you become a better witness? The motive behind this book is to encourage you to become a better witness by furthering your relationship with the King of kings and Lord of lords. Be bold and not ashamed of that relationship. Study to show yourself approved and share the knowledge with others. Remember to pray and ask the Holy Spirit to open opportunities to tell the story of salvation. God loves all of mankind and wants them to be saved. Sow the seeds or water and fertilize the seeds already sown, God will reap the harvest.

SUMMARY

It is hoped that this section explained some basic Christian truths including:

1. The fact that there is a God and there is only one way to come to Him.
2. He offers salvation.
3. He sets the standards for right and wrong.
4. There is such a thing as sin.
5. There is a heaven and there is a hell.
6. Jesus is the Son of God.
7. There must be repentance if one wishes to be saved.
8. There is such a thing as faith.

We dealt mostly with the basics because execution of the basics is important if one wishes to grow into other and deeper understanding.

.

II

RELIGION AND GOVERNMENT, A SEQUEL TO CHAPTER 2

11

GOVERNMENT

You will notice that this section is titled Religion And Government and not Church And Government. The reason is that all government is based on someone's religion. The question is whose religion. Perhaps this section could be titled Civics 101 1/2, The Half They Didn't Teach You in School. I guess the first thing to do is define civics.

CIVICS

According to the dictionary **CIVICS** is that department of political science dealing with rights of citizenship and duties of citizens. From that definition it is apparent that we will be concentrating on the rights, duties, and responsibilities of citizens. Understanding civics is important. We will not get into details of how a bill becomes law but rather the broad view of government and its impact on religion.

One definition of my own is that politics, the political process, and government are three distinct entities. I call this the Unholy Trinity because in fact they are not a trinity but are taught and considered as if they are one.

We will discuss these entities in detail in the chapter on each one. Suffice it for now to say that politics does things indecently and out of order. The political process is the means by which one gets into politics or government. Government is established to see that things are carried out decently and in order.

In this country government is supposed to be controlled by the Constitution. I say supposed to be because we have three branches of the federal government that have ignored or misinterpreted the Constitution. Down through the years, people suffering under the yoke of monarchy, fascism, Nazism, socialism, and other forms of totalitarian slavery looked to the United States as a symbol of what could be. Those people understood, as they looked to America, that the Americans held one supreme advantage: America had a marvelous innovation, a written Constitution. That Constitution stood as a firm and unshakable rock, protecting the liberties of those lucky people who lived under it, binding and limiting even the most powerful member of the government. That Constitution could adapt to changing circumstances, but the real glory of it was that it could be changed only when the people themselves decide that a change is needed. It is the peoples' Constitution, it is not the government's Constitution. It is not in the power of government officials to ignore it as they see fit. It is not in the power of the black-robed judges or lawyers to change it as they deem proper. And it is written in plain language which the people can understand. It does not require the intervention of **legal specialists** or **judicial edict** to tell the people what their Constitution means. The Constitution guarantees freedom **of** religion, not freedom **from** religion. Treaties have the same effect in our lives as does the Constitution. We will examine treaties in more detail in a chapter by that title.

To some, the study of citizenship is boring and laborious. This book presents the subject in an interesting if not an exciting manner. Not only that, it is hoped that you will be inspired to take an active interest and role in governmental affairs.

There is a chapter dealing with the issue of church and state. Hint, there is an indissoluble bond between the gospel of Jesus Christ and our government. Nowhere in the Constitution can you find the term "separation of church and state." The first ten Amendments to the Constitution are referred to as the **Bill of Rights.** The first one deals with freedom of religion, speech, press, and the right to petition our government.

Most people have heard that this is a government of the people, for the people, and by the people. Who are the people? We are. Is government our servant or our master? Read on and judge for yourself.

GOVERNMENT

It was said in the introduction that Politics, the Political Process and Government are three distinct entities. We will talk about Government in this chapter. Webster's New Collegiate Dictionary gives 7 uses of the word government. None of the seven items say that the purpose of government is to see to it that things are to be done decently and in order. This book makes such a contention. See if you can detect anything indecently or out of order in the phrase "We the people of the United States, in order to form a more perfect union. Establish justice, insure domestic tranquillity, provide for the common defense, promote the general welfare, and secure the blessings of liberty to ourselves and our posterity, do ordain and establish the Constitution for the United States of America." With such a contention lets look at the purpose of government. According to Romans 13:1 all powers that are ordained are ordained of God. Therefore one can say that government is ordained by God. Civil government is covered in that we are to submit ourselves to every ordinance of man for the Lord's sake. The United States of America is subject to the Constitution of the United States and to God. In reading the Constitution one can only conclude that the purpose of that document is to insure that things are done decently and in order. The Declaration of Independence states that the government derives its just powers from the consent of the governed. This makes it look like our government was established by man and not by God. Lets look at this a little further.

NATIONAL GOVERNMENT

As stated before, the Constitution establishes the authority for the U.S. to have a national government. The founding fathers were careful to set up a checks and balance system. The Constitution sets up the Executive, Legislative, and Judicial branches of government. They wanted to establish a government that would serve the people rather than be a master over the people. With this in mind they stated in Amendment 10 that "The powers not delegated to the United States by the Constitution, nor prohibited by it to the States, are reserved to the States respectively, or to the people." Thus we see that the people command the government and not the other way around. If one were to review recent court decisions (Supreme and District) one might conclude that the government has the ultimate power over the people. This is not the way things are supposed to be in either the Constitution or the Bible.

THE EXECUTIVE BRANCH

Every organization needs a leader. The leader set up by the Constitution does not have unlimited authority. He has authority to run the Executive Branch and provide leadership but is supposed to be checked by another branch when it comes to doing something not granted by the Constitution. I say supposed to be checked because many Presidents have taken powers not granted by the Constitution without being checked by another branch. An example of this can be seen by examining Executive Orders. It seems that Presidents, with impunity, have violated the Constitution and treaties while other branches of government have stood by and not applied the necessary checks.

STATE GOVERNMENTS

Each state has its own Constitution. State Constitutions must not be in conflict with the U.S. Constitution. The chief Executive Officer of a state is the Governor. Each state has a state legislature and a judicial branch as well as an Executive branch. State governments have many duties but none infringe upon the duties of the national government. Their jurisdiction covers the geographic area of a state. The U.S. Constitution provides for adding new states. Thus we have gone from 13 to 50 states.

LOCAL GOVERNMENTS

County and City Governments take care of issues having an impact in their immediate area. Local governments are not immune from State and National Constitutions. Thus citizens have a lot of responsibility in keeping track of governmental affairs. It is true that freedom requires eternal vigilance.

CHRISTIAN NATION

Remember that at this time we are talking about the Constitution of the United States. A study by Baylor University found that 34% of the quotations in the Constitution came directly from the Christian Bible. The other 66% of the quotations were quotes from people who were quoting the Bible. Is this a Christian nation or not? What do you think? In looking at the preamble to the Constitution one can conclude that in order to secure the blessings of liberty one has to rely on someone other than man. Therefore one can conclude that our government was ordained by God. Sure the Constitution was written by humans but so was the Bible. Thus writing can not be equated with ordaining.

VOTING

Another thing, it looks like voting gives humans the right to appoint leaders and not to be raised up or put down by God. Lets look at voting. Some people pray before voting, others do not. Thus it seems that some people put God in the political process while others do not. Again in the matter of submitting onself to a higher power, one has to concluded the both the believer and the non-believer did the will of

God. Does the vote make government a master or a servant ? Thus voting seems to be part of the governing process. If one doesn't go to the voting booth one nevertheless votes for the winning candidate. The winner is happy you did not vote for the loser and influence the outcome of the election. Thus voting is one of the rights and responsibilities placed on those eligible to vote. And why do you vote? Is it because you want things to be done indecently and out of order?

PURPOSE OF GOVERNMENT

One of the main purpose of government is to see that things are done decently and in order. Our Constitution clearly state what some of those things are. Over the years our national legislature has expanded the role of the federal government beyond the items enumerated in the Constitution, or so it seems. God ordained government. Someone else ordained politics. More on politics in Chapter 12.

CHRISTIANS AND GOVERNMENT

Many people say that Christians should not be involved in politics. I agree with that statement. I believe Christians should be involved in government and not in politics. The current political climate is such that it is almost considered a crime for Christians to express an interest in the affairs of their civil government. We hear the statement that there is a separation of church and state. That is probably correct although not in the Constitution. At the time the Constitution was written church and religion were probably considered the same. However, it was never the intent of the founding fathers to deny the role of religion in government. Their intent was only to deny government sponsorship of any church or religion.

RELIGION AND GOVERNMENT

I think it is clear that religion belongs in government. All laws are based on some religious grounds. The question then is whose religion. As far as I know, all religion teach against murder, adultery, incest, steeling, lying, and other such things as part of their religious doctrine. Why then do some claim that this is a Christian nation. Earlier it was said that the Constitution quotes the Bible and not other books thereby making it clear that this is a Christian nation. Thus one can say that the Constitution mixes religion and government. Note that the statement does not contend that there is a mix of church and government. All that is contended is that religion is part of government. To emphasize the role of religion in our civil government I quote John Quincy Adams went on to say, "The highest glory of the American revolution was this: that it connected in one indissoluble bond, the principles of civil government with the principles of Christianity." The Constitution guarantees freedom **of** religion, not freedom **from** religion.

CHRISTIAN PARTICIPATION

I would like to quote Patrick Henry who said, "It cannot be emphasized too strongly or too often that this great nation was founded not by religionists but by Christians. Not on religion but on the gospel of Jesus Christ." I guess those who believe in the gospel of Jesus Christ also believe in the proper role of government. Thus Christians have a responsibility to participate in the operation of government. There are many ways to participate, some of which are listed below.

CHRISTIAN VOTERS

There are many organizations that encourage Christians to vote. In order to vote one must be registered. A voter should be informed in the issues and what the candidates believe as well as what a referendum will accomplish. (Not all ballots have referendums-only candidates-others have referendums only.) The matter then is how or for whom to vote for in elections. To be well informed one needs to pray, study the issues and candidate statements and seek the guidance of the Holy Spirit. The Bible clearly defines what is right and what is wrong. After the vote, one has to take note of the office holder's record and demand accountability.

CHRISTIAN PARTY MEMBERS

Most party organizations have some procedure for selecting party candidates. Usually there is a call for a meeting. Normally such a call will be publicized in newspapers or other new outlets covering the area. Active party members are well informed about meetings so it behooves Christians to be active party members. Christians have a responsibility in becoming active party members in order to have a grassroots impact on party activities. Decisions about party activities are discussed and voted on at regular meetings. The general public sees only the end results. Therefore if Christians wish to have a meaningful impact they need to be involved early on. Only by active participation at the grassroots and higher levels can Christians really make a difference. Christians need to fill precinct chairmen and other party positions. How does one get such position? First one needs to become an active party member. Second Christians need to show that they are human and care about the affairs of government. Third one needs to be consistent and be able to articulate issues and principles. Finally, one needs to be aware of all governmental activities ranging from local, city and county offices, state functions and national legislative affairs.

GOVERNMENTAL ACTIVITIES

I know that keeping up with all levels of government is asking much but we live in such a society and as such we need to be aware of things happening at every level of government. After all, it is a government of the people. Yes, we have a representative form of government. Does your representative represent you views? He or she will if you take an active part in the political process. At the national level we have the U.S. Constitution. Each state has a State Constitution. There is some kind of document spelling out the authority of a local government. A local government sees that things are done decently and in order at the local level. State government generally take care of things beyond the local level although it gets involved in some local affairs. The federal government among other things is charged with providing for the common defense, establishing justice, and promoting for the general welfare. Some federal administrators have interpreted promoting for the general welfare as a license to get involved in local activities. Another venue is the federal budget process. Thus we see the federal government involved in activities that are reserved for the several states or the people. Where in the Constitution does the federal government have the right to involve itself in education or the arts? We could point out many other areas where the federal government is involved on the pretense of promoting for the general welfare but all we want to do at this time is to point out a principle. We need to elect federal office holders who respect the limited role of the national government. People have give up many of their freedoms in exchange for security. It has been said that people who exchange freedom for security are not worthy of either. Thus the proper role of government is to see to it that things are done decently and in order.

DECENTLY AND IN ORDER

Throughout the old testament we see that in order to have success various leaders divided functions along orderly units. In looking at the Constitution of the United States one sees the provisions for things being done decently and in order. Starting with Article I, one sees that the legislative powers were orderly vested in the Congress of the United States. More will be said later about the various articles and amendments to the Constitution of the United States. Suffice it for now to say that the Constitution outlines a process that will insure that things will be done decently and in order. However, recent legislators and judges have done things indecently and out of order. Who can say that the national debt is decent? Who can say that some of the court decisions are in order?

GOVERNMENT, LAW, LOVE

It has been said that laws are useless unless they affect the heart. Thus law without love will not accomplish the government purpose. Ezekiel 36:26-27 states that God says "A new heart also will I give you, and a new spirit will I put within you: and I will give you an heart of flesh. And I will put my spirit within you, and cause you to walk in my statutes, and ye shall keep my judgments, **and do them.**" (Emphases mine.) We see then that just passing laws does not change the heart. Only God can change the heart. Most Christians do not see the authority given government as a threat. Nor do they see imperfections or gross errors in government as reasons not to pray for the leaders. The true Christian is not a bystander in electing those who are in government. In reality Christians should be in the thick of battle for justice, morality, and the character of those in government.

Christians look for justice but that involves making judgments on certain issues. Thus many say that Christians are intolerant. Not so! They just would like for people to abide by the rule book and stay in bounds. What if the wasn't a rule book? The government's rule book is the Constitution. The rule book for Christians is the Bible. Thus the motive of Christians for justice is not negative. They simply agree with what the Bible says is right and wrong. There are absolutes. For this they are labeled bigots or worse. In fact, some of the people who call Christians intolerant and wish to portray themselves as tolerant do not tolerate Christianity. It is apparent that government law without love is useless. Government can pass all kinds of laws but unless the heart is changed the laws are useless. A murderer is breaking both moral and legal law. Obviously his heart is not governed by the law. We see people murdered after a rule has been handed down that the murderer is not even supposed to see the victim. A lot of good such rule has if it has not affected the heart. Neither the law nor a rule stops the murderer. This is but one example of where laws are useless. I'm sure you can come up with many other examples. The point I'm trying to make is that only a change of heart will make moral or civil laws effective. So much for the power of government.

12

POLITICS

It can be said that politics is an imitation or counterfeit of government. Government is ordained by God and politics by someone else. The politician is interested in promoting himself rather than the good of society. He will promise everything to everybody and will say anything to get or keep the office. There is a distinct difference between politicians and statesmen. The matter of statesmanship will be addressed later. For now we will look at politics and politicians.

POLITICS

It was stated earlier that politics does things indecently and out of order. Lets look at some indecent acts of politics. Is there any doubt that the national debt is indecent. How did such a indecent national debt occur? It can safely be said that the debt came about because politicians promised many goodies without paying for them as costs for such goodies were incurred. Is this solely the fault of politicians or do the voters share some of the blame? By passing the cost to our children and grandchildren it looks like the present generation is getting something for nothing. Nothing can be further from the truth. Notice that the national debt keeps growing even when there is a "balanced" budget. This is politics using smoke and mirrors to give us a good feeling. It will take a long time before "balanced" budgets reduce the national debt. I wonder if our children and grandchildren will feel good about the present generation of politicians leaving them holding the bag! Can it be true that there is no such thing as a free lunch?

Another indecent thing that politics is doing is taxing us at a rate not contemplated by the Constitution. It has been said that local, state and federal taxes amount to over 40% of what some people earn. True, we get lots of services for our money. Who isn't happy to have streets, roads, national defense and other essential government services? Politics has extended the word "essential" to include many "wants" and not just "needs."

POLITICIANS

Now to go from politics to politicians. Politicians according to Webster's New Collegiate Dictionary is "one versed or experienced in the science of government." The second definition is "one addicted to, or actively engaged in, politics as managed by parties; often, one primarily interested in political offices or the profits from them as a source of private gain." There are two significant factors in such a definition. The first talks about one versed or experienced in the science of government. There is little doubt that a politician is versed in the science of government. The trouble with that is the second factor. The politician is interested in the private gain rather than the gain of society.

POLITICAL OFFICE vs. GOVERNMENT OFFICE

A politician is interested in political office rather than governmental office. Earlier it was stated that politics is a counterfeit of government. Politics use the political process to gain political office. We have been brainwashed into believing what I refer to as the "Unholy Trinity." I refer to government, politics and the political process as the "Unholy

Trinity" because the three are three separate entities instead of one and the same. I have already addressed the subject of government in Chapter 11 and now in Chapter 12 I am addressing politics and by extension politicians. Chapter 13 will address the political process.

POLITICIAN vs. STATESMEN

We have been led to believe that politicians fill government positions. The statement of political office aptly describes the office of a politician. Notice that politicians are primarily interested in private gain and public gain is incidental to their own gain. Statesmen on the other hand occupy governmental offices and benefit when the public gains. This pretty well defines the differences between politicians and statesmen.

13

POLITICAL PROCESS

UNHOLY TRINITY

Now we come to the third entity of what I have called the "Unholy Trinity." The political process can be equated with a job application. The political process is used to get into politics or into government. Although there are many political parties in the United States, I will address the political process as if we had a two party system. Coalition governments around the world have not been as successful as the "two party" system. The political process enables individuals to get into the "two party" run for office and get elected. Some individuals pursue government office through some party other than the two major parties but seldom get elected.

CHRISTIANS AND THE POLITICAL PROCESS

Christians have by and large stayed away from the political process because they didn't want to be involved with "worldly" affairs. God got involved in "worldly" affairs when He created the world. More will be said about Christians and Church and State in Chapter 16. Suffice it for now to say that Christians should be involved in the political process. It has been said that all that is needed for evil to triumph is for good to remain silent. For too long Christians have been silent about governmental affairs. Christians, like everyone else, have a responsibility to be involved with the political process. Many Christians claim that politics is the sewer of society and them when they get in politics the sewer becomes their personal hot tub. This is why I say that I agree with the statement that Christians should not be involved with politics. They should use the political process to get involved with government and not with politics.

GOVERNMENT OFFICE

As stated before, political office and governmental office are not the same. Political office is held by a politician. A government office on the other hand is occupied by a statesman. The work done in each office may be much the same but the motive is different. The politician looks at the work and analyzes how he can profit from legitimate activities conducted by that office. A statesman on the other hand looks at how society can benefit from the activities of a governmental office.

14

THE U.S. CONSTITUTION

Although this chapter looks at the Constitution, it is not a legal interpretation. For that I urge you to read the Constitution and consult a Constitutional lawyer. However, a lawyer is not needed to interpret the Constitution. More is said about this when I review Amendment Number 6. I will look at Articles, Sections and Paragraphs. The Constitution starts out with a preamble which reads as follows: *"We the people of the United States, in order to form a more perfect union, establish justice, insure domestic tranquillity, provide for the common defense, promote the general welfare, and secure the blessings of liberty to ourselves and our posterity, do ordain and establish this Constitution for the United States of America."* We conclude from this that what follows insures the orderly and proper conduct of the government.

ARTICLE I

Section 1, plainly states that the legislative powers shall be vested in the Congress composed of the Senate and House of Representatives. (As of late the Judicial Branch, in the form of the courts including the

Supreme Court and some lawyers, have been making laws rather than limiting themselves to interpreting the Constitution.)

Section 2, paragraph 1 specifies the qualifications of members of Congress.

Paragraph 2 establishes the minimum age of a representative, a citizen of the United States and an inhabitant of the State in which he or she shall be chosen.

Paragraph 3 talks about the raising of taxes and the count of voters. Modifications on the raising of taxes and counting people were made by the 14th and 16th Amendments.

Paragraph 4 addresses the issue of vacancies.

Paragraph 5 provides for the selection of a speaker of the House and vests the power of impeachment in that body.

Section 3, paragraph 1 establishes the Senate, specifies how many senators each state shall have and Amendment 17 modifies the Constitution to provide that the people rather than state legislators will elect senators.

Paragraph 2 specifies how vacancies will be filled.

Paragraph 3 addresses the issue of qualifications for a Senator.

Paragraph 4 provides that the Vice President of the United States shall be President of the Senate.

Paragraph 5 states that the Senate shall choose their other officers.

Paragraph 6 assigns the Senate the sole power to try all impeachments. The last paragraph of this section sets the punishment of one found guilty as a result of the trial held per paragraph 6.

Section 4, paragraph 1 establishes the time, places and manner of holding elections.

Paragraph 2 states that the Congress shall assemble at least once in every year.

Section 5, paragraph 1 states that each House shall establish the qualifications of its own members.

Paragraph 2 says that each House shall make its own rules.

Paragraph 3 provides that each House shall keep a journal of its proceedings.

Paragraph 4 places limitations on adjournments.

Section 6, paragraph 1 agrees that the laborer is worthy of his hire.

Paragraph 2 says that no Senator or Representative shall serve in more than one office at a time. In most states lawyers are part of the Judicial Branch of government and thus should not be elected to any other branch but they are.

Section 7, paragraph 1 states that all revenue bills shall originate in the House. (There is at least one case where a court ordered a jurisdiction to spend federal funds. It seems to me that the Judiciary Branch originated a revenue bill.)

Paragraph 2 states how a bill becomes law.

Paragraph 3 states that every order, resolution or vote, except on a question of adjournment, shall be presented to the President. A veto by the President can be overruled by a vote of 2/3 of the Senate and the House of Representatives.

Section 8 has 18 paragraphs listing the powers and duties of the Congress. Read the Constitution to see what the powers and duties of the Congress are listed.

Section 9, paragraph 1 deals with migration or importation of certain persons. (Slave trade, not prohibition by congress prior to 1808.)

Paragraph 2 provides the privilege of the writ of *habeas corpus*.

Paragraph 3 sees to it that no laws are made *ex post facto*.

Paragraph 4, amended by the 16th Amendment, provides the authority for the federal government to lay and collect taxes.

Paragraph 5 states that there will be no export tax by any State.

Paragraph 6 prohibits commercial preference of one State over another.

Paragraph 7 establishes that the Treasury can only dispense money per enacted laws.

Paragraph 8 maintains that we will not have any titles of nobility.

Section 10 has 3 paragraphs which deny certain powers to States. (Read the Constitution for further information.)

ARTICLE II

Section 1, paragraph 1 vests the executive power in the President.

Paragraph 2 which was superseded by the 12th Amendment sets up the procedure for electing the President and the Vice President.

Paragraph 3 establishes that the electors, in paragraph 2 as amended, shall vote on same day.

Paragraph 4 establishes the qualifications for President.

Paragraph 5 sets up a procedure for a successor in case of a vacancy in the office of the President.

Paragraph 6 provides for compensation for the President.

Paragraph 7 establishes the Oath of Office for the President.

Section 2, paragraph 1 makes the President Commander-in-Chief of the armed forces of the United States.

Paragraph 2 gives the President the authority to make treaties (More on treaties in Chapter 15) with the advice and consent of the Senate, grant pardons, make certain nominations and appointments.

Paragraph 3 gives the President the power to make appointments during the recess of the Senate.

Section 3 provides, among other things, for what is now known as the State of the Union.

Section 4 provides for the impeachment and removal from office for all civil officers upon conviction of treason, bribery, or other high crimes and misdemeanors. The definition is not resolved.

ARTICLE III

Section 1 sets out the Judicial powers, tenure, and compensation.

Section 2, paragraph 1 establishes the area of Judicial power and as modified by the 11th Amendment states the jurisdiction of the court.

Paragraph 2 gives the Supreme Court original jurisdiction in all cases affecting ambassadors, and other specified cases.

Paragraph 3 establishes trial by jury except in cases of impeachment.

Section 3 paragraph 1 defines treason.

Paragraph 2 gives the Congress the power to declare the punishment for treason.

ARTICLE IV

Section 1 provides that States shall give full faith and credit to public acts, etc. of other states.

Section 2, paragraph 1 as amended by section 1 of the 14th Amendment provides that the due process of law shall apply to all citizens. I don't want to discuss amendments at this time but section 2 of the 14th Amendment forces me to go there at this time. Section 2 of the 14th Amendment has a bearing on what was said earlier about the 12th Amendment.

Paragraph 2 provides for the returns of persons charged with a crime from one state to another.

Paragraph 3 as modified by the 13th Amendment addresses the issue of involuntary servitude.

Section 3, paragraph 1 provides for the admission of new states.

Paragraph 2 talks about Congressional power over territory or other property to the U.S.

Section 4 guarantees every state a republican form of government.

ARTICLE V

This article provides a method of amending the Constitution.

ARTICLE VI

This article has been modified by section 4 of the 14th Amendment which has been mentioned above. The article states that the Constitution and Treaties shall be the supreme law of the land. It states that oaths to support the Constitution is required of certain officers.

ARTICLE VII

Article VII states that ratification is required to establish the Constitution. The Constitution consisting of a preamble and seven articles was adopted by a majority of the delegates attending to Constitutional convention. The Constitution was then ratified by the participating states. Three states had a unanimous vote and the other ten had a split vote but nevertheless enough votes needed for state ratification. There was opposition because the Constitution failed to explicitly provide for individual and state rights. This led to an agreement to present certain safeguarding amendments after the adoption of the Constitution. Twelve amendments were submitted and ten were adopted. The ten became known as the **Bill of Rights.** There have been 27 amendments since then with one amendment repealing another. Some people think it is time for another Constitutional Convention. Should we change the Constitution or our attitude towards the original document? I will now briefly discuss the amendments.

AMENDMENTS

(Not all sections cited herein-to view all sections read the Constitution.)

ARTICLE I

The first amendment deals with freedom of religion, speech and press. It also guarantees the right to petition the government. As stated earlier, we are guaranteed the freedom **of** religion, not freedom **from** religion. The first amendment prohibits the government from establishing a national religion. All laws are based on some religion. The question is whose religion. As pointed out earlier many of the quotations in the Constitution are taken directly or indirectly from the Christian Bible. Therefore as stated before the author contends that this is a Christian nation!

ARTICLE II

This article provides for a well regulated militia and for the right of the people to keep and bear arms. Much has been made of this provision. Some say that it is all right to keep and bear arms so long as those people are part of the militia. Others say that the commas separating the right to keep and bear arms from the rest of the sentence clearly indicates that people do not need to be part of the militia to keep and bear arms. (The author is of the latter opinion.)

ARTICLE III

This article places responsibility on the federal government for quartering its soldiers.

ARTICLE IV

This article insures the right of the people against unreasonable search and seizure. (One's home is one's castle.)

ARTICLE V

This article insures that no one will face double jeopardy. It also provides that the government will pay just compensation for private property taken for public use.

ARTICLE VI

This article provides that an accused shall enjoy the right to a speedy and public trial. It also guarantees that the accused shall have the assistance of counsel. (Notice that the word is counsel and not lawyer. The legal profession has led us to believe that the word counsel means lawyer. However, the dictionary makes a distinction between the two.)

ARTICLE VII

This article guarantees the accused shall have the right of trial by jury.

ARTICLE VIII

This article prohibits excessive bail or fines and cruel punishment.

ARTICLE IX

This article guarantees the rights of the people. (Remember earlier it was said that there was opposition because the Constitution did not explicitly provide for individual rights. This remedied that situation.)

ARTICLE X

This article addresses states rights. (It overcomes the objection mentioned above.) (On September 25, 1789, Congress transmitted to the state legislatures 12 proposed amendments. Two were not adopted. The remaining 10 amendments became the **Bill of Rights** and are considered the same as the original Constitution.)

ARTICLE XI

This article modifies paragraph 1, section 2 of Constitutional Article III regarding the exemption of states from suits.

ARTICLE XII

This article superceded paragraph 2 of Constitution Article II regarding the method of selecting the President and Vice President.

ARTICLE XIII

This article abolishes slavery.

ARTICLE XIV

Among other things amends the original Constitution Article IV, Section 2, to clarify the protection of citizens rights.

Section 2 of this article specifies the apportionment of Representatives in Congress.

Section 3 gives Congress the right to remove certain disabilities of potential candidates.

Section 4 declares certain debts valid.

Section 5 gives the Congress the power to enforce these provisions.

ARTICLE XV

This article gives equal rights for all citizens to vote.

ARTICLE XVI

This article amends the original Article I, Section 9, paragraph 4 to provide for the imposition and collection of income tax.

ARTICLE XVII

This changes Article 1, Section 3, paragraph 1 of the original Constitution to specify that Senators will be elected by the people of a state rather than selected by the state legislature. It also specifies how vacancies to the U.S. Senate will be filled.

ARTICLE XVIII

Prohibits the manufacture, sale, or transportation of intoxicating liquors. The only amendment repealed by another amendment. (See 21st Amendment)

ARTICLE XIX

Provides for nation-wide woman suffrage.

ARTICLE XX

Establishes the dates for the beginning of the terms of the President, Vice President and the Congress.

ARTICLE XXI

As mentioned above, this article repeals the 18th Amendment.

ARTICLE XXII

Sets a two term limit for anyone occupying the office of the President.

ARTICLE XXIII

Section 1 states that the District of Columbia is the seat of Government of the United States and states the number of electors the District shall have.

Section 2 states that citizens of the District of Columbia have a right to vote for President and Vice-president.

ARTICLE XXIV

Section 1 states the Vice-president becomes President in case the President leaves office for any reason.

Section 2 provides that the new President with the consent of the Congress shall appoint a new Vice-president.

Section 3 provides a way for the Vice-president to take the place of the President for a temporary time if the President so indicates to Congress.

Section 4 gives Executive Departments or such other body as Congress may by law provide the right to declare that the President is unable to carry out his or her duties and then the Vice-president becomes President and provision for deciding who shall act as President

ARTICLE XXV

Defines Presidential Disability and Succession.

ARTICLE XXVI

Section 1 gives people at the age of 18 the right to vote.

Section 2 states that the Congress shall have power to enforce this article by appropriate legislation.

ARTICLE XXVII

Provides that pay raises for Senators and Representatives shall not take effect until after an election.

This is a short review of the U.S. Constitution and its Amendments. As stated before, this is not a legal interpretation nor are all sections of the Amendments cited. It merely reviews the document as any citizen is entitled to review it. One thing that is wrong with our government mentioned earlier is that there are too many lawyers serving in other than the Judicial Branch. The legal profession has become the law maker, the interpreter and the administrator. This is not how it is supposed to be. Lawyers write ambiguous laws which then have to be appealed thus putting more money into the pockets of lawyers. If a non-lawyer tries to offer counsel and interpret such laws they are charged with practicing law without a license. I suppose if ordinary citizens try to interpret the Constitution they can be accused of practicing law without a license. Yet interpreting the Constitution is everybody's right. Having ordinary citizens run the government leads to a limit on the power of the federal government. I say this because as I interpret it, the federal government has assumed powers not granted it by the Constitution and the legal profession has not objected to usurpation of states and people's rights. In effect, some people think the Constitution is not worth the paper it is written on. Some people think the Constitution is outdated and should be revised. A few think it has served us well and all that is needed is a change in **attitude** to agree with provisions of the Constitution. The author agrees that we need a change in **attitude.** I don't think you need a lawyer to change attitude.

15

TREATIES

My research although based on solid empirical study did not tell me how many Treaties are in effect. However, it did lead me to believe that many Treaties are not worth the paper they are written on. If you don't believe this statement, ask some Native Americans. It seems that might makes right when it comes to honoring Treaties and the U.S. Constitution. He who has the power dictates the term of the Treaties, breaks them when convenient and honors them when such is to his advantage. U.S. Treaties cover the range between what will be done between states and nations, taxes, the military, etc., as shown below. Supposedly when a Treaty is not ratified by the Senate it does not go into effect. I say supposedly because recently a Cabinet Member wrote a letter on behalf of the President to several heads of state stating that the U.S. would abide by the terms of a Treaty it had not ratified.

TREATIES ACCORDING TO U.S. CONSTITUTION

As stated in the review of Article II, Section 2, paragraph 2, the President shall have power, by and with the advice and consent of the

Senate to make Treaties. Further Article VI, paragraph 2, states that all laws and all Treaties made shall be the supreme law of the land. Some of the Treaties infringe on the sovereignty of the United States. Are these Treaties Constitutional and legal since they have the power of the law of the land but violate the sovereignty of the U.S.?

TREATIES

Among the many Treaties I reviewed for this book were those dealing with: Business and Economy, Society and Culture, Military-Arms Control, International Law, Environment and Nature including Climate, Indigenous people, Taxes, Copyrights-Trademarks, Indian Wars, Human Rights, Intellectual property, Crime-Prisoner Transfer, etc. I doubt that even a lawyer versed in Treaties can tell us exactly how many are in effect. Even those agencies charged with administering Treaties probably can't get an accurate count of what is in place and those that have been violated. Treaties are part of the laws of the nation. However, the nation seems to violate its own laws with impunity.

16

CHURCH AND STATE

"Congress shall make no law respecting an establishment of religion, or prohibiting the free exercise thereof;..." This is part of the First Amendment. The government has placed strong emphasis on the "establishment" portion of the amendment but has been almost silent in the "prohibiting the free exercise thereof." It has gotten to the point where a teacher or a student cannot display a Bible even though it is not interfering with the school mission. In terms of some administrations a Bible is as dangerous or more dangerous than a gun. The term "Separation of Church and State" is nowhere to be found in the Constitution. It is true that state and church should remain separate entities but that doesn't mean that the state is free of religious influence. Notice that "religious influence" is not the same as "church influence." While it is not the purpose of this section is to explore the difference between religion and church suffice it to say that the two are not the same. The point is that all government law is based on somebody's religion. Again I say whose religion? There is no such thing as government remaining neutral when it comes to religion. Neutrality advocates of atheism believe in neutrality but that is somebody's belief and therefore meets part of the definition of "religion."

STATE

One of the definitions in my Webster's New Collegiate Dictionary is that a state is "A political body, or body politic: any body of people occupying a definite territory and politically organized under one government, esp. one that is not subject to external control." The United States qualifies as a state under that definition. Further the authority of the U.S. government is the Constitution. This makes the point that a state is not a church.

CHURCH

The International Bible Dictionary states in part that "The Greek word translated church signifies generally an assembly, either common or religious..." I have chosen the "religious" connotation because of a definition of "religion" below. In fact, a building has come to be recognized as a "Church." With that in mind we see clearly that the state and church are two separate entities. Neither entity is to rule over the other according to the U.S. Constitution. This provision gives us freedom **of** religion, not freedom **from** religion. Actually the church is the body of Christ and not a particular building or denomination. The Good Leader Bible says that from "Apostolic TIMES the church has been REGARDED as a brotherhood or FAMILY, not a promiscuous GATHERING of believers and unbelievers. The SERVICES were at FIRST held in the HOMES OF MEMBERS. (Rom. 16:3-5; Col. 4:15; Philem. 2.) Thus again one can say there is a definite difference between church and government.

SEPARATION OF CHURCH AND STATE

In a letter by Thomas Jefferson to a committee of the Danbury Baptist Association in the state of Connecticut he stated with regards to the government prohibiting the free exercise of religion "building a wall of separation" between state and church. From that letter sprang the doctrine of separation of church and state and not from anything in the U.S. Constitution. In fact, the U.S. Constitution in effect prohibits there being a "Church of the United States."

RELIGION

We have defined "Church." Obviously there is a difference between church and religion. Webster's New Collegiate Dictionary defines religion in part as "The service and adoration of God or a god as expressed in form of worship." This is not a place to go into the intent of a capitol G versus a small g or God versus a god. Suffice it to say that a capitol "G" and the word "God" refer to the creator of the universe while a small "g" and "a god" or "gods" refer to pagan gods. Service and adoration of God is not the same thing as salvation. Church and religion can not offer salvation. Only God can offer salvation because of His mercy and grace. Religion, on the other hand, can offer a pseudo peace while the gospel of Jesus Christ offers a peace beyond understanding. The founding fathers apparently referred to religion and Christianity as interchangeable. Do not confuse "religion" with "spirituality." The Holy Spirit is concerned with spirituality and not religion.

DENOMINATIONS

Many people have the mistaken impression that denomination and church are synonymous terms. I believe that God gave someone a revelation and that someone started a denomination around that revelation believing that this was the *only* way to get to heaven. God saw that the revelation was not the total picture so he gave someone else another revelation. That someone else started a new denomination. Each believing that by doing things according to that denomination's doctrine one was coming to the "true" church. Neither realized that there was unity although not uniformity in such ventures. Only God could see across denominations and the fact that there is unity in the gospel of Jesus Christ. That is the explanation of the author as to why there are many denominations in Christianity. By this rational one can extend the definition of religion to conclude the many races are one race of humanity. Thus I conclude that there is only one "true" race and that is the human race regardless of color or nationality.

17

BRANCHES OF GOVERNMENT

This chapter talks about the various branches of government. They are discussed here in the order listed in the U.S. Constitution. The order of discussion is not to be interpreted as the order of importance but rather by the function and relation to each other. The founding fathers wanted to set up a system of checks and balances so that no one branch of government dominated the organization. This concept has been carried over to all levels of government.

LEGISLATIVE BRANCH

One of the earliest documentation of law was given as the ten commandments. Humankind has since written a bunch of laws. Chief among them is the Constitution of the United States which sets out broad guidelines for conduct of society in the U.S. (See Chapter 4.) The founding fathers favored a government of the people, for the people and by the people. The government was to be a servant of the people, not its master. Article 1 of the Constitution establishes a Legislative Branch consisting of the Senate and the House of Representative.

These two houses are to present to the President proposed laws which govern the conduct of the national government. Such laws, signed by the President, clearly are to be constitutional. Another branch of government is to see if in fact the laws are constitutional. More will be said about this branch when we discuss the Judicial Branch. Every state and local government has a legislative body of some kind.

EXECUTIVE BRANCH

Article II establishes the Executive Branch. As mentioned before, every organization must have a "head honcho." The head guy for the U.S. is the President. He has a bunch of helpers. This is known as the cabinet consisting of heads of various executive agencies. The President, through executive orders and other Presidential documents, directs the operation of the executive agencies or what is known as "the government." The executive agencies issue regulations based on legislation and actually implement the laws. Some executive orders go beyond directing agencies and in fact exceed the President's rights under the constitution. This seems to be OK with the other two branches. There is no doubt that an Executive Branch is necessary to the orderly conduct of governmental affairs. However, voters need to pay attention to what this branch does. Voters elect the head honcho and thus have a say on how that office operates.

JUDICIAL BRANCH

Article III of the Constitution establishes the Judicial Branch. Article III vests the judicial power in the Supreme Court and in such inferior courts as the Congress may from time to time ordain and establish. Such courts are to interpret whether laws enacted are in fact in accordance with the Constitution. In recent times the courts have legislated through their interpretations and have not been checked by the other two branches as provided for by the Constitution. Thus the Judicial Branch has become the dominant branch of government. As stated before, the only thing wrong with law is lawyers. Not all lawyers are of this ilk but many in doing their job end up legislating.

As stated before, the concept of three branches of government is carried out at the state and local level. At the state level there is a Governor, State Legislature and a system of Courts. Local governments call their chief executives names ranging from Chairman of an organization, mayor, city manager, and other such titles. Then there is some kind of a legal branch.

INDEX

Abortion	31	Article XII	109
Abortion Options	32	Article XIII	109
Abraham's Bosom	51	Article XIV	109
Alive	27	Article XV	109
Amendments	106	Article XVI	109
Article I	101	Article XVII	110
Article II	104	Article XVIII	110
Article III	105	Article XIX	110
Article IV	105	Article XX	110
Article V	106	Article XXI	110
Article VI	106	Article XXII	110
Article VII	106	Article XXIII	110
Article VIII	108	Article XXIV	110
Article XIX	110	Article XXV	110
Article X	108	Article XXVI	110
Article XI	108	Article XXVII	110

Backing Up To Find Life	26
Baptism	35
Basics	77
Bible, The Word Of God	7
Bible Versus Guns	21
Biblical Hell	52
Biological Birth	55
Biology	30
Born Again	57
Boundaries	19
Branches Of Government	15
Changes In The Constitution	16
Christian And Believer	43
Christian And Non-Christian	42
Christian Foundation Of U.S. Government	15
Christian Nation	89
Christian Participation	14
Christian Party Members	92
Christian Principles	19
Christian Voters	91
Christians And Government	14
Christians And The Political Process	99
Church	116
Church And State	115
Clockwork	67
Coincidence	73
Civics	85
Coming To God	4
Comments About Heaven And Hell	49
Continued Logic	9
Constitution For Godly People	20
Corruption And Incorruption	41
Creation Or Evolution	71
Day Of Return	40
Denominations	117
Decently And In Order	93
End Time	43
Enough Is Enough	6
Error	60
Evidence of Resurrection	8
Executive Branch	120
Experience	22
Faith	78
False Doctrine	36
False Teachers	37

Father	57	Judicial Branch	120
First Bag	73	Justified By Blood	43
Fire And Brimstone	50	Legislative Branch	119
Flesh And Spirit	28	Legislative Process	26
Free Moral Agents	68	Life Begins At Birth	25
From Death To Life	27	Life Begins At Conception	29
Gender	10	Life Before Conception	28
God	58	Local Governments	89
God Intervenes	71	Logic	8
God Is In Contro	73	Lost And Saved	63
Godly Laws	20	Love	59
Good Works	11	Man Created	68
Government	87	Mark Of The Beast	44
Government Office	100	Master Or Servant?	17
Government, Law, Love	93	Mentioning Christian Beliefs	21
Governmental Activities	92	Mercy And Grace	12
Grace	64	National Government	88
Heart Beats	29	New Life	26
Heaven	47	One Lord	34
Headwind	72	One Way	11
Hell	49	Participation In Government	23
Is There A God?	3	Political Office vs. Government Office	96
Jesus The Only Way	11	Political Parties	16
Jesus The Son Of God	6		
Jesus Will Return	40		
Judgment	5		

Political Process	16
Political Process	16
Political Process, Not Politics	17
Politicians	96
Politicians vs. Statesmen	97
Politics	95
Predestination	70
Purpose of Government	13
Religion	117
Religion And Government	22
Reward And Punishment	52
Reverend	60
Robots	69
Salvation	6
Searching For Fulfilling	76
Second Look At Male And Female	59
Separation Of Church And State	116
Short Run, Long Run	19
Sin And Salvation	77
Sodom And Gomorrah	37
Spiritual Birth	56

State	116
State Government	88
The Egg	34
The Firmament	48
The U.S. Constitution	100
Thousand Year Reign	44
Torment	51
Treaties	114
Treaties According To U.S. Constitution	113
Tribulation	39
Trinity	36
Trinity Not Found	33
Twinkling Of An Eye	41
Unholy Trinity	99
Unity In Diversity	63
Unity Is Not Uniformity	62
Upper Case And Lower Case Letters	56
Voting	89
Where Is Hell?	50
Which Trimester	28
Works	78

ABOUT THE AUTHOR

He is married and has a son and a daughter. He is a veteran who served in Korea. He is a graduate from the University of Colorado. In his walk with Jesus he has taught Sunday School, led a prayer group, served as Treasurer of a church. He was baptized more than 30 years ago.

ABOUT THIS BOOK

This book is not the light but there is material that bears witness of the light. One of the purposes of this book is to help Christians with their witnessing. The book points out several scriptures that address questions raised during the many conversations cited. Perhaps you will encounter some of these questions in your witnessing. The answers mentioned in this book always cite scriptures which address the issues. A second purpose of this book is to wet the appetite of non-believers to further research.

9 780595 011179